'Some say it's brave men who speak truth to power, but in this book braver men speak truth to self. *MANDEM* is ground-breaking for real, and it's not just for the mandem. It's for the greater good. These writers illustrate in the most lyrical, poetic, and intelligent ways, that there is a lot going on outside, but there's more going on inside.

I recommend that all human beings read this book. It enlightens.'

— Benjamin Zephaniah

# MANDEM

## edited by Iggy London

JACARANDA

This edition first published in Great Britain 2023
Jacaranda Books Art Music Ltd
27 Old Gloucester Street,
London WC1N 3AX
www.jacarandabooksartmusic.co.uk

A CIP catalogue record for this book is available from the British
Library

ISBN: 9781913090944
eISBN: 9781913090951

Cover Design: Dowon Jung
Typeset by: Kamillah Brandes

*To my family, for giving me the words to write and the confidence to never stop.*

# CONTENTS

# CONTENTS

# Mandem United

## Iggy London

**THIS BOOK IS NOT JUST FOR THE WOKE. THIS BOOK IS NOT** just for the politically correct inner-city creatives living in Shoreditch's trendiest apartments. This book is not just for the people who listen to podcasts and are well-versed on speaking about the effects of gentrification and the cost of living crisis. Your chakras do not need to be aligned for you to understand this book. You don't need to have a PhD in Social Theory to relate to this book. This is because this book is not just for those who identify as intellectuals. It is not just for the young men and women of the snowflake generation who know what 'hyper-masculinity' is. This book is not just for Black men who feel comfortable wearing fuchsia or pink or velvet—I know there are many of us. Shout out to my fellow brethren. This book is not just for my mother who probably found it easier to shut this book than to open it. Although she probably would never say it out loud. Shout out to you too. This book is not just about masculinity. It is not strictly about class, race or religion. This book is not just for the mandem.

This book is and will forever be a book for the people. The book that seeks to challenge what society views as what is an important story to tell and what isn't. This book is personal. For those who read this, you should all know that this book is about lived experiences, ones that will remove the tight ring that holds a lot of men (and women) to believe in the stereotypes referenced herein. And Lord knows I have had to learn this the hard way. Cue story time.

1993. Cold as fuck. Victor and Esogie, both Nigerian nationals, migrated to England with hopes for prosperity and peace. The pair passed across thousands of miles to finally call western civilisation their home. With history so densely packed in their suitcases, they sat on their long haul flight, anxious as to what could possibly await them when they landed. Although happiness coated their memories, so did disaster and frankly London was a way out of war into peace—into certainty.

My mother, Esogie, an owner of a small clothing store in Edo state, and my father, Victor, a tailor, each had big ideas of what this new world would provide for them. Eventually the pair would settle for the second floor of a council estate building in East London instead. Too frightened to integrate, they built their own fortress of Africa in the heart of their home. Maggi cubes, scotch bonnets and an assortment of spices would flood the nostrils of visitors walking through our corridors. Windows firmly closed for fear of letting out the smell of difference.

I was born on 15 May 1994. Enveloped by the Little Nigeria my parents created in the comfort of our council flat, this would define what I understood to be home. As a child agility was my best friend as I studied each vital step to the stove, removing the steaming hot lid and picking up the leftovers of my mother's newest delicacy. Barely brave enough to hold it in my hand for two seconds, I would eat at the bottom of the stairs, being careful not to scorch myself.

The youngest of five girls, my mother would pay close attention to the way she looked. After she finished cooking, I would sit on her bed and watch her bring down her suitcase from the top of her faux marble wardrobe—the finest furniture from Upton Park market. I'd stare as she rummaged through a plethora of African cloth. Finally satisfied with a modest number that covered everything but her ankles, she'd wrap her waist with the remnants of her last remaining connection to the motherland.

With a stern glance at me, I would quickly put on the shirt my mother prepared for me, fit for the lie we were about to present. The bell sounded and the show began. I leapt down the stairs, peeking through the holes in the bannister to see which family we were performing for today. A feeling of indignance remained from the last family we entertained. My father sat in the living room as my mother would greet people, who looked like senators and noblewomen.

They would exchange words and phrases: 'Welcome', 'God bless you', 'We thank God' and 'God bless you', as if they were playing a game of who could be the most holy. At such a young age I realised how important the facade was for my parents. They needed to build this everlasting idea of what Nigeria looked like to them in case they ever forgot.

Like many others growing up in Newham, there had been no formal invitation to the other quadrants of the city and so for most of my adolescence 'the ends' was the only place that mattered. Pre-2012 Olympics, the inner-city borough was predominantly a working-class area with a large Black and Asian community.

There were only two buses that took me and my brothers right opposite the school gates. Over here, we always sat at the back. Music always blasted from brick phones sat perfectly on window ledges to address their audience. The 'olders' never spoke, they just did. In Newham, MCs were respected over singers. Kickers over Wallabees. Ski masks were worn even though no one had been to the Alps.

I don't know when I realised that men like me were not afforded the luxury of emotion. I don't remember when I first realised that men like me had a certain role to play. I arrived at this misnomer not by any miraculous vision or intellectual enlightenment. No, I learnt this from Newham. Looking back on my experiences, growing up in Newham as a young kid was an incredibly awkward time for me.

Newham was a place where most boys thought they had to be strong men before they were fully-fledged adults and, admittedly, I was one of them. Newham was a place where we appeared ordinary but inside there was a reluctance to share ourselves completely with the outside world. I began to realise that humanity did not take into consideration the Black male state. We were not included in the big worlds of feelings, love, loss, pain, or joy in any meaningful way. More often we were completely excluded.

So I, like many of my peers, adopted the standard archetype of the 'no-emotion-big-man'. It was this framework that boys who looked like me had to live by if they were ever going to be praised as men. And if we didn't obey these Draconian rules that were imposed on us from our inception, we were instantly labelled as an 'other'. It is sad to say but for the longest time, I believed this dogma and acted accordingly.

By the age of 16, my pubescent self was more confused than ever. It was safe to say that hypermasculinisation continued to be imposed on me. Cue flashback:

It is a non-uniform day and the product design students are working on their coursework. Product design is a class

I thoroughly enjoy but pay no attention to because staring at the laser cutter is far more engaging than knowing what polymethyl-methacrylate is used for. I pre-planned my outfit perfectly; a white Primark t-shirt, a Topman slim-fit flowery shirt and black skinny jeans topped off with some tanned boat shoes—harmless I thought.

I quickly found out that this outfit wasn't part of the 'hood man starter pack'. The olders came for me first. The gay jokes started from the playground and slowly worked their way through to first and second period. The questions came after.

*'Fam, what the fuck are you wearing?'*

*'Why the hell are your jeans so tight? Are you a girl?'*

It took me a while to realise that my own authenticity couldn't exist in this *Grand Theft Auto* world that I was being told to live in. But I couldn't just drive off a bridge in San Andreas and respawn into a wiser, stronger version of myself. Instead, I just rolled with the punches. Life taught me that the person I aspired to be wasn't the type of man the boys at my school wanted to be. I chose to subvert the 'norm' and to construct my own identity.

Fast forward to present day and it appears that for many of us, masculinity does not live in such archaic confinements anymore. You've got men dancing on TikTok and eating kale and taking pictures on Instagram stories using puppy dog filters. Masculinity is not as fragile as it once was—I think.

Fortunately, there is no one way to define masculinity or manhood. Why? Because there is no one way to be a man in this new modern landscape. I mean, what would be the benefit in having another framework to call 'normal'? Think about it. The same historical frameworks that were created for men to uphold were given as goals to achieve and aspire to—a masculine measuring stick if you will. Not only are these definitions tiresome to the modern-day man, but some men might feel they do not fit into these narrow categories. We have evolved further than these labels. If I had to describe what a man is to an unclassified foreign life-form from Mars, I would say simply, speaking coherently in its cool alien language:

'A man is a person who takes consideration of his many facets and does not limit himself to a specified few; whether that be through his emotions, his behaviour and the way he responds to social pressures, his thought-process, or his reasoning— all whilst bearing in mind his own position in society amongst women.'

I strongly feel that with the obvious struggle to achieve gender equality and since investing in discussions on feminism that are further advancing our understanding of the sexes, there has been more of an open conversation about what masculinity means and whether the rigid, stereotypical dimensions of masculinity have any space in this day and age. And I hope they don't because I can't go back to screw-facing people on the bus for no reason and practising my best Darth Vader voice.

In so far as conversations surrounding masculinity go— it is a peculiar time, one that warrants the need for this book. On the one hand, the recent rise of the 'manosphere' understandably has led to growing concerns about how we as a society understand and speak about masculinity. Yet at the same time, as a society we have gotten better at addressing certain representations of masculinity as well as dispelling ancient ideals that have dictated how men should behave or feel.

It is imperative that our conversations about masculinity and manhood continue to evolve in an honest and healthy manner. In order for such dialogue to be effective, men need to have spaces to speak about their issues. We need to facilitate conversations where men are given the right to be open and vulnerable.

It wouldn't be right to introduce this book without speaking about the authors who inspired my ideas, thoughts and consequently gave me the courage to also write down my own story. bell hooks was one of the first writers I came across. Her book *We Real Cool* is a heartfelt plea to Black men across America to radicalise their own consciousness and to challenge patriarchal masculinity. Despite the advancement of the feminist movement, sexual and gender liberation, bell hooks made it clear that men have yet to take accountability for their own lives and until they do this, they will be victims of their own oppression and policing.

Although eloquently written and perfectly posed, bell hooks's book, understandably, offers no real commentary on the lived experiences of men in the UK. Popular conversations about masculinity have always been Americanised, limited to perspectives and experiences within the confines of American borders. A lot of good has come from this. In recent years, we have witnessed the rise and development of contemporary conversations, literature and insights surrounding the experience of men within the UK. This book, I hope, will be part of that.

This book has been designed for the sole purpose of giving you a beautiful glimpse into the infinite plurality of the Black male experience. But it is important to note that this book is not a portrait of all the types of Black masculinity. There is no one way of being a man. There is no one way of being Black and there is no one way of being a Black man.

The rigid and harmful expectations that come with being a 'man' become even more heightened when our Blackness is included. Race plays a huge part in this conversation of masculinity, to ignore it does a disservice to the conversation.

Imagine being a carefree Black boy. Your parents have

always told you that you could be anything you put your mind to—an astronaut, a robot, a cardboard box. You always believed you had the right to decide who you wanted to be, for yourself, and on your own terms. Suddenly, your mum and dad come home from work one evening and come into your room whilst you're typing away on MSN and listening to Tinie Tempah's 'Wifey Riddim'.

They make you turn off your music and sit you down to tell you that you are no longer allowed to believe you are free. You are no longer the controller of your own destiny. When you are a Black boy you become, in the eyes of many, the person *they* want you to be; a caricature of yourself. The colour of your skin dictates your narrative more than your intellect ever could. You are no longer allowed to be the person you are. Black men are racialised, criminalised and fetishised, but never realised.

And to the men of colour who are reading this book and can relate to the strict confines that have been placed upon us, what I am about to say to you is what I had to learn for myself. If this isn't your first-time reading this then it's fine, but if this is, I am sorry it has taken such a long time.

# Mandem United

Remember:

You do not need to hold back your tears when watching *The Lion King*.

You do not need to hide your asthma pump in your sock in fear girls will feel sorry for you.

You do not need to wear two jackets in the club just to present yourself as a non-perspiring strength of steel.

You do not have to like whiskey or drink a bottle of Stella Artois every weekend to represent yourself as one of the lads.

You do not need to be strong to be a man.

You do not need to know how to sweet talk the ladies to be a real man.

You do not need to be a roadman to be a 'real' man.

You do not need to listen to trap music to be a man.

You do not need to be born a man to be a man.

I urge every Black man to create a mantra like this for themselves. I know this book cannot speak for all Black men. I don't think this book and books alike can single-handedly put to bed the toxic caricatures, stereotypes, expectations that have led to the chaos we see today. But I do hope this book can be the catalyst for getting men to walk boldly and fearlessly through a door that has routinely been closed. I believe that the stories you are about to read will spark interest, conversation, maybe a campaign, a panel discussion, a hashtag, a speech, which will hopefully contribute to the cultural shift we so desperately deserve.

Remember, it starts from us—the mandem—speaking up.

# Birthday Cards

## Yomi Ṣode

**I ALWAYS PICTURE THE INTRO SEQUENCE FROM** *BELLY* whenever I think about myself and the mandem's entry into clubs. Ask me in my 60s and it will be no different from my 20s. The first four minutes of Hype Williams's directorial debut as a filmmaker are undeniable. A confident head nod, daring the doubters to talk smack about him or his work, and maybe that's what continues to stand out to me. The power. '*Oooooh-ooh-oh-ooh, ha-ha. Steady, are you ready? What's going on?*' Caron Wheeler guides us in as the Black car pulls up at the strip club. The line plays almost like a call to arms as Sincere, Tommy, and Mark get out of the car and start walking past the queue of people waiting to get inside. The camera snaps from the car as it leaves to Tommy, lighting a cigarette. His shoulder soon embraced by Sincere as they walk towards the entrance. Chains swinging from side to side, their leather jackets, a size or two bigger to make room for their egos. The bouncer lifts the velvet rope to let them enter as Tommy looks almost guiltily at him. If you look close enough, you'll notice a boy wearing his baseball cap backwards, watching Tommy in awe as he makes his way in. *'Cold fresh air, feel the melody that's in the air.'* There's a bop in each step, a Manorism in the way that Sincere scopes his surroundings, navigating the landscape as the camera continues to pan in slow motion to Tommy, Mark and back to Sincere, as they stand, still in the club. You feel their presence in that moment. The ultraviolet light luminating their bodies as they walk towards the dancers. Knowing what eyes have followed them to that point. *'However to you want me, however do you need me?'*

2015 was an unrelenting year.
2015 gave me JME's 'That's Not Me',

Stormzy's 'Know Me From',
Skepta's 'Shut Down',
and Kendrick's 'Alright'.

2015 followed its predecessors with the murders of Walter Scott, Freddy Grey, and Sandra Bland. It seemed like my back was facing the mirror that 2015 was holding up to me, waiting the longest time for me to turn but I was anxious in doing so, mainly because I had no clue what the mirror was asking of me. I tend to escape through my phone though, I knew that once I dipped into the random banter with my boys it could suppress the guilt of feeling useless.

Talking shit with the mandem felt like a safe haven. Talking about anything to break away from realities I had no control of.

Backaday, the plan to get into NYT was simple.
I finished work around 4pm:
I'd get home,
eat,

> sort out what to wear,
> wait a couple hours then
> leave in time to jump on a bus 12 to Oxford Circus.

If you're lucky, the conductor won't come your way. If you see him coming? You hop off and wait for the next one to arrive. A standard procedure. Just to note that this type of clever broke in winter was very long! Once I reached Oxford Circus (around 7pm,) I'd link the mandem and we'd walk into Trocadero for a bit to kill time. Drinking our bottles of coke, mixed with Jack Daniels (that we could never handle) in haste, switching on the faux machismo whenever the girls walked by. Our opened shirts begging to be looked at while knowing we were fucking freezing. By 9pm, we were waiting in line rushing to make it in before 10pm because clever broke knows the difference between free entry, and £10! Our shivering bodies weren't going through all of this for nothing. Our shirts were oversized, we wore work and (in some cases) church trousers with shoes that no one could judge in the dark. Shoes that had you running out as the lights switched on. Yeah, the plan was simple, get in the dance, get the numbers and leave before everyone else does.

I lived out some of my best years in clubs. I remember Pharrell's 'Frontin' as my permission to seduce with a voice that wasn't quite Maxwell. A voice that wasn't too off pitch to sound fucked. I'd sing, *'Don't wanna sound full of myself or ooooo'* for three years not knowing this guy was saying *'rude'*. But mandem knew the magic in an Usher side step and a silent mouthing of *oooo* was like fairy dust blown from our right palm. This one line was whimsical and transient, it was eyes locking amid darkness splattered with ultraviolet light, catching all of our imperfections. Fluff and deodorant stains on our shirts, our smiles, the only way of not losing each other to the night. I danced until my shirt stuck to my skin, making it unbearable for girls to touch or hold me at times. I willy bounced, signalled the plane and Harlem shaked. I was silly and sinning every week. Content to be at an age where responsibilities felt less heavy. We got a bite of NYT and craved for more. Whether Cameos, Moonlight, or Bar Rhumba. Cameos, with the predatory bouncer that cast us aside while making way for girls to enter. The same dickhead bouncer making us wait longer while other, more important men walked in. Men not having to queue, men like Sincere or Tommy, men with money looking at us as they made their way in. Taller, broader, baller men, leaving us like scraps to join after. I'd remember walking in and avoiding the gaze of these men, later walking out like *that won't happen to me, to us again.* And so we responded. Church trousers changed into Valentino or Evisu jeans, jackets changed into Avirex, shoes changed to Prada, leaving our bank balances looking like wilted flowers. None of us ever speaking about it. None of us ever discussing the urgency of getting our gym memberships due to the taller, broader men we saw in the club. But we still met in front of the club, at the same time, after taking the same journey, in our new clothes with aching arms, feeling warmer—with emptier pockets to tuck our hands into.

On September 3rd 2015, I sent the following message to my boys in our WhatsApp group.

*Yeah. It's a tricky one. I still hold the fact that nothing keeps friends going more than honesty. Like I'm more than prepared to say and share my thoughts knowing that you may not like it or that you may think differently of me but, at least it's out there. True story, I watched* Straight Outta Compton *last week. After the film finished, me and Nat are walking out, I spot this group of breddas coming out of the cinema as well and I was like 'I've never done that with my boys.' Then shit got deeper. Never bought you man bday cards or a present on your birthdays or Christmas. Sounds stupid but these things matter. These are what proper friends do like. It has to be more than the odd raves here and there, feel me?*

My expectation was for them to feel me but maybe I expected too much. Maybe what I was asking for, at the time, was for them to listen different (hold tight Tshaka). Maybe what was underpinning this sudden revelation was a notion that I had yet to grasp. Though I wasn't laughed out of the room or told to stop smoking whatever I was high off, I was somewhat simmered down with *just know we are good, and that presents don't define friendships*. But I was struggling to see how nights of outings and drunkenness made us closer.

December 4th 2006. I'm sat with the mandem in our allocated table in Shadan's nightclub in Blackfriars. I would realise more and more as years went by, how lacklustre the VIP allocated ting is. I would also realise that this shit is THE fastest way to watch your drink ferry itself into the liver of clever broke people. Though those days were over, we could spot our past selves without fail. This night in particular felt different. It was a Sunday, and raves on a birthday, it's not like we did not celebrate it the night before at Silks n Spice in Bank and what a night that was. So this felt a little forced, but we made the most of it, leaving our allocated space as the DJ warmed the crowd onto the dance floor, we got going. Mandem can be hype, there's a language to it though. A Manorism, and to some degree an ethical code of alpha maleness that comes with it. Something chemical maybe. The key part is in the prediction of how it could be triggered, and the unpredictability of how bad it could get. Aside from the bouncer at Cameos being a predator, he purposely upped the ratio of women in the club to decrease the risk of any altercations between men happening. A flawed, objectifying and misogynistic theory then and now but something I've witnessed over the years, as well as Black men being refused entry week in week out. Black men getting out of their cars, walking up together then splitting up in the queue as though they are strangers. This goes from prevention of violence, to targeting, stereotyping and, well, racism. The chosen few made it through. Hence our additional celebration in knowing the luck in actually making it in until of course, the celebration stops.

I stood next to a guy, who I would later know was named Ola, as the mandem shouted 'Happy Birthday'. And he turned to me saying, *'Your birthday yeah? It's mine too, bro'* and though we were strangers, we embraced to entering our new age, together. Pouring refills into our empty glasses, dancing like fools until parting ways and returning to our respective groups. As I've gotten older, I learned that I'll never be able to freeze time. Not the time Shortie was laid flat on the ground, already beaten halfway to death and the guy then swinging his boot, clocking him whilst still unconscious. Not the time the punch came from nowhere and all I did was hold the angle from where it came, grabbing the shirt, pulling him downwards shouting *prick* and swinging nonstop, knowing my head was still reeling from the sucker punch but also knowing that opening my eyes would have me in a worse state. All I had was the muscle memory of violence reminding me to just swing until he gives or I am pulled from him. Not in time to tell Olu to back up or say sorry to the guy's creps he stepped on. There was still time between my man looking at his creps and up at Olu, I thought. Time for dialogue. But Olu is drunk and it's his birthday and I've seen this movie too many times. A man too waved, coming across like he doesn't care, pissing off the other man that wants to be taken seriously, now looking like a prick in front of his crew. All hell broke loose on the dance floor. Screams were heard. The lights flicked on. It all felt like a movie. In fact it felt like the opening scene in *Belly* after the gaze towards the dancers, and Sincere, Tommy and Mark walk into the ladies bathroom, retrieving their guns. It's at that point I clocked that there was more to this outing. This no longer was about three men wanting to have a wild night out but rather, a night that's about to take a turn. I watched intensely as the three men pull their ballies down and rush up the stairs, shooting the first man in sight that's blocking their way, entering the room with such force, holding their guns in a sideward slant and shooting everyone in the room.

Their arms outstretched pulling the stacks of money across the table. A motion akin to windscreen wipers, watching a waterfall of bundles tied with rubber bands drop into duffle bags, soon dashing out of the club like the group of boys that ran up the stairs, leaving Olu in the middle, standing on a white ceramic dance floor with blood gushing out of him. His blood. So much blood. It did not stop pouring. Olu looked up at the exit, all fight in him, like he could still do something to the boy that stabbed him with glass. Olu's leap towards the steps soon slowing down and I was scared. Finally, we were allowed to leave the club and as we walked out, we saw him, lying flat on his back. Olu died that Monday morning, December 4th, our birthday.

Olu Olagbaju. The newspaper described him as a God fearing man and father. I left my boys that morning and I walked from Blackfriars to the Aylesbury Estate, which wasn't any safer but it was home. My mum was awake when I arrived to wish me Happy Birthday. She was surprised that I wasn't drunk, and still relatively dry. She could even still smell my Versace Blue Jeans like I was readying to leave. I wanted to tell her I saw a man die. It's not like I haven't been in proximities of death before. I've been close enough to duck from or hear the thud of bottles smash over a man's head. Close enough to hear what I hoped was a pop of a motorbike exhaust, causing the panic of people running, and seeing no motorbikes. Close. I wanted to tell her he was Nigerian, and that it was his birthday as well. I wanted to cry a cry for him, I wanted to pray a prayer for him, I wanted her to pray for me but I said nothing. Not that morning, or afternoon, with countless missed calls on my phone, not even the evening a week or so after when I received a call from the police to come in for questioning. The sparse green room with two white men sat opposite asking questions as though I was linked to both groups of men; *We were both out with our people celebrating our Birthdays. That was the first and last time I saw him.* The look in their eyes had a 'but all Black people know each other' thing about it. In hindsight, It was a silly move to attend that alone. I didn't tell my mum because a parent's fear was something I already understood, something I wanted to protect her from. The Christmas period loomed and I was out with the mandem again as though a murder didn't take place just a few weeks before. This was how we mourned. We drank knowing one of us still had to drive the majority home. We spoke to girls trying to convince ourselves that this is what Men do. You spend, you show out, you drive, you VIP, you flirt, you fuck, you brawl. You don't listen to that inner voice telling you who you really are, or why the hell you are doing what you are doing.

The last ever message in the WhatsApp group from …. is dated December 30th 2014. It reads

*Guys, tomorrow is going to be busy as fuck for me so I'm saying this from now. Happy New Year. Whatever you guys do, hope you have a good 1.*

Five days after that message, he went out, got drunk and lashed out in a way that's now costing him 18 years in jail. When it came to attending his trial, there was hesitance in the group. One could argue and say *'Nah those ain't your boys! If that's your mandem? You ride through the good and bad times.'* But this was something different. Sometimes you can hang out with people who share common interests and know nothing of each other at all.

I'm a sucker for reality TV. I like to think there's something to take from watching the lives of others.

*Love Island, Four in a Bed, Come Dine with Me*, the list goes on. So picture my excitement when a new show is premiered, titled *Rich Holiday, Poor Holiday*! Two families or groups of friends (upper and working class) swap holiday budgets and location. The upper-class group of friends are given £1000 to manage as a group, while the working class group had a budget that had them looking at each other with much confusion, in a good way. The only challenge for the working class group, was their setting for the week. A health retreat that involved no booze or greasy food and a week of yoga, meditation, and healthy eating. A nightmare for the working class group. I wouldn't have minded being in this situation with my boys but with … in trial it opened the can of worms that had stayed shut for so long. The dance, the drink, the girls, always being the escape from ourselves. And this situation served as a detox, the same way the health retreat had the working class group hold the mirror to each other in regards to their friendship. The anxiety was real, and I was angry at my boys, wondering how we couldn't stand behind plexiglass so that he could see us, somehow. There was no denying it, he killed someone but there's more to this, surely? I was angry, but we have never been here, dealing with this kind of reality. Drunken hugs are different from actual hugs, and a night out does not mean you've actually listened. I thought I was listening until a string of mental health incidents pertaining to my friend reeled off the tongue of his barrister in court. All the while I'm thinking to myself, *but we've known each other since we were 11 years old.* There would be no more outings as a group for a while. Some messages here and there and a breakdown, the tipping point in the autumn of 2015.

On the face of it, it seems pretty stupid to suggest to mandem, let's go bowling rather than rave. Though I think at the heart of it is my anxiety regarding my proximity to danger. It's

Blackness not only being a target of whiteness, but also from itself, like the guy that stabbed Olu, and I was tired of readying my body for battle. Some dangers just can't be avoided, but should something kick off, there might be a sigh of relief knowing it's in a space that's well lit and has 80s pop hits for a change. And maybe all of those deaths in 2015 had me like enough is enough.

I really wanted to talk about the murders, racism, BLM, the police. I wanted to attend a march and not think of what suit to don in a dance. Maybe I was never given the space in the group chats or I never created the space in the group chats to interrogate something that was really important to me. The last time we went out as a group was in 2019. I missed us but it didn't feel the same. Of the mandem that's left, we looked around at this landscape and how x amount of years ago we would rush to be the first people in. We cringed at the bredda in the muscle top sat under the AC acting like he couldn't feel the cold, we looked at breddas in the shadows, whose hands would come out every once in a while. At one point, we thought that was smooth, but we grew to realise it's insecurity in not knowing how to dance or approach women correctly. We looked at each other, paused, laughed and said *fuck, we are old!* Now when I ask '*How are you, bro?* and met with *I'm here, bro. Just trying to be like you! Man like..* And 'here' continues to be the space we live in. How long until this house finally rots?

# Get Rich or Die Tryin

## Athian Akec

### BLACK MEN DEAL WITH TRAUMA BY GETTING RICH.

To be young, Black and working class is to live a life that places riches at a higher priority over everything else. For many of us, money is the only answer to our present and future hurdles in life.

When we wake up, we think of it. When we go to sleep, we dream of it. In the UK, we are fixated on stacking 50 pound pink notes characterised by the stoic expression of Queen Lizzie. For those in the US, they imagine the iconic image of Benjamin Franklin on crisp green paper glaring at them. The list goes on. Country to country. City to city. Black men stay married to the quest of attaining it. The prospect of flexing it. Iconic rap lines have been born from the motif of it. From Nas's 'I'm out for dead presidents to represent me' to Kendrick's 'money trees is the perfect place for shade' and Nines's 'don't talk money if it's less than a mil,' these words read like captivating poetry to many Black men. If I went into just how many rap songs explore, mention, celebrate the need and desire for Black men to get money—we would be here for forever.

So why are we so fixated about the idea of wealth and obtaining it? There are layers to understanding this phenomenon. Let's start with mental health.

There is a clear link between unaffordable rent, the slashing of benefit payments, inflation and mental health issues. So why don't we hear about this when we speak about mental health? Part of it is because people in power are resistant to the systemic change that would be needed to address these issues. It's easier to keep the conversation in the place it currently is. So for us to grapple with understanding why as Black working class men we may feel like *getting money* is a way out of our trauma, we must acknowledge the impact of things like wages, security and access.

Then there is the media. Where does one even begin? Unless you have never watched the evening news or picked up a newspaper, you too will know when it comes to how the media depicts Black men it is often rooted in violence. During the height of the 'knife crime epidemic' between the mid 2010s to 2020, the British media, particularly the tabloid press, framed the issue often by using tropes of 'black on black' crime as a justification for the widespread return of stop and search policies against young Black men. Research done by the British Journal of Criminology published in 2018 titled 'Does Stop and Search deter crime? Evidence from ten years of London wide data' found that there was no link between the use of stop and search and the reduction in crime. In an interview with rapper and author Akala on *Good Morning Britain*, Piers Morgan asks Akala a peculiar question:

> '...this is predominantly a problem of young Black boys who are almost exclusively part of gangs attacking each other so that the perpetrators and the victims are almost exclusively young Black men. Do you think there is a racial element to that? Is there any cultural issue, racial issues or do you think it's the same problem they had in Glasgow where they were white. And that is actually the race part of this where we may look at the statistics and think this is a Black problem when it's actually not?'

Akala in all his brilliance goes on to dispel the myth that the youth violence happening at the time was driven by race, more specifically violence. He then highlights the causes of violence across the world namely school exclusion, relative poverty and domestic violence.

Black men, like all humans, are not beyond confrontation. But rarely ever is the violence inflicted upon us by this society's institutions talked about. It's well established that violence between people and groups has an impact on people's mental health. Rarely is it ever acknowledged that the trauma rooted in society's violence against young Black men has a part to play in this. To understand our trauma you have to understand the forces that shape the lives of Black working class communities. The root of the problem is the violence inflicted upon us.

The Windrush deportations and the Grenfell Tower fire are two recent events that have tragically shaped the way we view the world specifically as it pertains to race and class. Events such as these live in the collective psyche of young Black working class people. In the case of the Grenfell fire, that day served as a flashpoint for how the powerful in this country disregard the lives of people like *us*. From a mental health lens, it highlighted a few things.

**NUMBER ONE:** How we are constantly dehumanised and seen as less than.

**NUMBER TWO:** The inability of mental health services to support us.

**NUMBER THREE:** How the realities of migration, a flawed education system and absurd economic inequality make life for the working class almost impossible.

According to mental health charity Mind, although Black men and white men experience mental health issues at statistically similar rates there are disparities in certain conditions. When it comes to psychosis for example Black men are ten times more likely than white men to be diagnosed with the condition. When it comes to clinical decisions, preconceived negative notions of Black manhood dictate how we are treated within mental health institutions. Research conducted by Mind shows that Black people's interactions with the mental health system are more likely to be violent and defined by the use of force. The statistics are shocking—here are just a few:

*Black people are 40% more likely to access mental health treatment through police or a criminal justice route.*

*Black people are less likely to receive psychological therapies.*

*Black people are more likely to be compulsorily admitted for treatment.*

*Black people are more likely to be on a medium or high secure ward.*

British society is unequal. At the core of British society is the principle of meritocracy. The original concept of meritocracy was written by Michael Young in the late 1950s as a critique of elites who used narrow definitions of merit to justify their elevated position. Research done by academics at King's College London has shown just how central to the British collective consciousness the idea of meritocracy is. A survey conducted in February 2021 looked at what factors people thought were most important in people's success and the results show just how clear people in this society entertain the idea of meritocracy as how power, money and resources are distributed. It concluded that in people's perception of the factors responsible for our success, 'hard work and ambition are perceived as the most important determinants of success. Three-quarters of respondents believe that hard work is essential or very important for getting ahead in life.' But evidence suggests that the link between merit and success is tenuous. The government's 2019 Social Mobility Commission revealed that Britain is far from a meritocracy, proving that in most cases the outcome of our lives is decided before we are born. The report concluded, 'babies born into disadvantaged households are more likely to have low birth weight due to poorer maternal diets and higher rates of inadequate antenatal care. This is then associated with worse health outcomes later in life. By the age of five, inequalities are clear: in 2018, only 57% of children with access to free school meals reached the expected level of development compared with 74% of children not entitled to free school meals.' In short—the idea that Britain is a meritocracy is a lie.

Our lives as Black British people are often defined by a myriad of dualities. Here's one. On the whole Black people, particularly those my age, are typically socially liberal, favouring intervention by the state to tackle social issues. However, while we don't largely subscribe to ideas of meritocracy, our understanding of what my community calls 'Black excellence' sounds remarkably similar to ideas of meritocracy. Generally speaking, Black excellence is a cultural phenomenon that has taken root in the social media age in which Black achievement has been pedestalised and is a particular form of heightened pride rooted in celebrating Black people who achieve in the context of the exclusion that we face. In this sense, Black excellence can be seen as the synthesis of meritocratic ideals we see in Britain and the glorification of a specific kind of success namely financial, academic or fame based. One dynamic that has birthed this phenomenon is undoubtedly an absence in the nuance in narratives around the success of certain young Black people. The Black British working class experience is multifaceted and has intricacies that are often erased within the rags-to-riches framework. Black excellence makes the mistake of overstating the importance of hard work and talent while erasing how much social mobility has to do with cultural capital, the school you went to or even pure blind luck.

This nuance becomes even more worthy of note when we realise that more often than not, the range for Blackness is to either be a complete failure or to be exceptional. This also begs the question—what does this do to the psyche of Black people? Existing in this context is both challenging and unhealthy.

So, how does the concept of Black excellence relate to Black men trying to get rich? Well, almost everything. Black excellence, Black exceptionality is a lens that many of us use to construct the world. Our experiences and external notions of Black excellence drive the kind of thinking that leads us to think we can deal with or bypass our trauma by getting rich. As Black men we view achievement, status and success as a shield from our early experiences in life that hurt us. In this case financial success is the ultimate armour against all losses.

This kind of pressure did not start with us. As Africans from across the continent, the 'hall parties' that defined our childhoods were equipped with glossy songs, sharp attire and high ceilings—all of which were an act of performance. A declaration of humanity and our freedom. An indication of our desire to achieve higher heights. A parading of our identity and hopes. At these hall parties, our parent's dominated the afternoons of opulence in the midst of the gritty difficulties of regular life. I don't think this spirit has left us, in fact it has been heightened by the newfound and developing possibilities of what life can look like. The realities of the past never die; they only evolve. From the fact that there are social media pages dedicated to documenting the designer drip of celebrities to how most parties are full of more cameras than dancing. To the distorted conversations about wages that happen on Black Twitter on a regular basis that don't match up with the economic reality of our community. It's clear that the spirit of performance is living on through new generations.

Earlier I quoted a few rappers and their famous lyrics about attaining money. In many respects, it is almost impossible to speak about the Black man's pursuit of paper without referring to rappers. This is for many reasons:

**NUMBER ONE:** Black male rappers often are representative of Black exceptionality in that they usually come from challenging, adverse backgrounds and have worked hard to attain fame and money, becoming the exception to the rule.

**NUMBER TWO:** Black male rappers often centre the attainment of money as an important part of their identity.

For so long, rappers have not just been a representation of heightened versions of the Black male performance, Black male wealth and Black male desirability, they have been *the* only representation of all the above. Since hip hop and its variations globally have become mainstream forms of artistic expression, rappers have existed as the dominant representation of Black men in the media and culture more broadly. This means for Black boys, rappers are the blueprint for Black masculinity. This is tied directly into the phenomenon of Black men dealing with trauma because typically the bars and hits that captivated the world have often been defined by materialism. This combined with the mainstream desire to consume Black culture has caused many rappers to become the patron saints of consumerism. This undoubtedly has had an impact.

The conversation about rappers and money is often—like most conversations about Black men and Black people more broadly—devoid of empathy and context. While acknowledging that it's important to remember that no one is above criticism, rappers must often feel like there is a pressure to play the role of being relentlessly consumerist but there's layers to this phenomenon. Many of my favourite rappers' most materialist works are their hits. These bangers are designed to travel far and wide to take their music into the mainstream and to ensure that their music hits the kids. The golden generation of British rap that we are witnessing have used catchy materialist bars to propel their songs into charting hits.

The discographies of these musicians go much deeper than that; their music at moments can powerfully critique everything from the issues ranging from systemic racism to the hypocrisy of the criminal justice system. On his song 'Handle it' from an early mixtape, Nines raps, 'I'm on trial, how theses juries and feds judge me, they can't relate cause they ain't never been to bed hungry,' and J Hus on his similarly early work asks this society about the criminalisation he faces, 'But why you wanna call me a criminal? You invaded my ancestors' land.' Here these rappers show how their music can play the role of social critique and political commentary. But the question is for the young Black men who seek guidance and leadership from these rappers, do these songs that educate compensate for the moments where they are flexing on us with worldly possessions we could only dream of affording?

Experiences of poverty in our mind, because of the absence of money, heighten the importance of money. And for good reason—growing up in London means to grow up in the context of the extremes of wealth and poverty. It is to live not that far away from people who have everything and people who have absolutely nothing. In more parts of London than not, right next to forgotten and neglected estates, are million pound houses and streets that drip with wealth. The wealth is hyper present and tauntingly close yet so far away. In London wealth is next door yet so out of reach. While we might hear about and understand these systems spoken about in newspapers or on TV reports they don't feel as real as the streets paved with gold that we walk past every day on the way to catch a tube or bus.

So does getting rich actually help with combatting trauma? Or does it just bring out our trauma even more? In trying to answer this question it's important to bear in mind how many of us actually 'get rich'. The world we live in as young Black men is one of inherently limited opportunity. While there are exceptions to this rule, the dominant experience of young Black men is one where we are excluded from opportunities to advance in life. Research done by the *Guardian* newspaper found that last year in some parts of England the rates of school exclusion for Black Caribbean pupils was six times higher than for white students. For Black students who make it to university the obstacles don't end there; research done by the Office for Fair Access found that Black students were 1.5 times more likely to drop out of university than their White or Asian counterparts. For Black men who chose other parts of advancement such as a career in sports or the arts these are high risk endeavours where the rewards are, despite what perception may have us believe, not fairly distributed between people and institutions. For every Black man who has become a millionaire off of music, there are people who are not financially prospering. For every Black man who has become a millionaire off of football, there are hundreds more who are released from academies every year who did not have any other life plans.

A report done last year by Warwick Business School on behalf of the government found that Black businesses were more likely to have their loan applications rejected. The point I'm attempting to communicate here is that as Black men, from working class inner-city communities, most of our paths to wealth are blocked and the psychological strain we are putting ourselves under to get rich in the middle of this context is real and has a cost. This makes me wonder, bleakly, if our obsession with getting rich is compounding the issues and traumas that we already have.

Improving our material conditions ultimately does not remove trauma or help with alleviating it. Even if we walk through the fire of all of our life experiences—the violence of poverty, the violence of social exclusion, the violence of growing up with parents whose lives have been changed by migration and escaping these conditions the way that they have shaped us—it doesn't suddenly change who we are. Years of wealth, usually reached in our late 20s or early 30s, cannot reverse psychological weathering of decades of poverty. The crushing weight and pressure of not having money in an expensive society does not lift suddenly when you achieve material success. Bleak memories are not erased by shiny floors, foreign whips and nice holidays (no matter what your favourite rapper might tell you). Memories of overdrafts and council letters that threaten to shatter your world don't suddenly disappear if you become wealthy.

We have to actively interrogate our ideas of what we think wealth will do for us. Will it alleviate our trauma or allow us to act upon our worst destructive impulses?

The experiences that shape us have so many impacts on our behaviours. The coping mechanisms we have in the face of these issues are not always healthy. The truth is getting money can simply deepen and enable this behaviour.

The point of this essay is not to be a critique of Black men or to invite pity upon us but to shine a light on a phenomenon that we see all around us. It's an argument for us to think about fulfilment, excellence and ambition in a different way. I want this essay to serve as a starting point for new possibilities of what we can do with our time, energy and resources.

This essay has been me providing perspectives and what I think are under-recognized truths but maybe it would be best to close with a series of questions about building a world.

How can our generation of Black men build a world where there are healthy ways for young Black men to truly deal with their trauma? How can our generation of Black men work to not only build power on an individual level but also on a more communal shared level? How can our generation of Black men, in the idealised depictions of Black masculinity, elevate the traits of fighting for justice, compassion and community above solely the virtues of power, wealth and status?

# The Pink Frame

## Sope Soetan

*'Tell these black kids they can be who they are.'*
**—TYLER THE CREATOR, 2017.**

*'No one wants to be the negro swan.'*
**—BLOOD ORANGE, 2018**

*'Pynk is the truth you can't hide."*
**—JANELLE MONAE, 2018**

**SEVEN YEARS OF AGE. THAT'S HOW OLD I WAS WHEN I WAS** almost lured to the permanent investment of a false self. No doubt it was fundamentally self-destructive, but at the time, I thought it was necessary. I had to do it in order to live an inoffensive existence. One where I could blend in and not be the odd one out.

Memories of that watershed day are hazy now, but I'll try my best to recollect them. I was in primary school. I remember everyone in my class was to have a picture taken of themselves. We would then be given an accompanying photo frame to decorate however we saw fit. Instantly, I was enamoured with the prospect because it was an opportunity for me to be creative. Knowing that I had such free rein enthused me.

I decided to paint my frame pink and further accent it with white flowers. I simply did what felt natural to me. Ample time was spent perfecting it, tending to its needs and making sure it was the best it could be.

But the world of escapism I was whisked away to while working on it was disrupted when I heard a male classmate utter something. The exact words I can no longer recall but I know it was an utterance of objection. A public damnation attempting to shame me for choosing that depraved colour.

According to my fellow seven-year-old, it was imperative that I change my design, as it was not suitable for boys. Unbeknownst to me, I had broken an unwritten code. Defying a rulebook that at the young age of seven, I was expected to be well-acquainted with and abide by.

The dogma that certain practices and tastes were solely meant for girls was already embedded in my classmate's still-growing psyche. So embedded that he had enough vigour and certainty in these sentiments to police me on the matter. He was adamant that there was a limit on the way young boys like us could express themselves. Anything outside of that unaccommodating cloak of masculinity was a transgression, punishable by chastisement and communal degradation.

You may be wondering how I responded to my pink

frame's rejection. Did I cower and concede to the pressure? Did I react in prideful anger? Not at all. Though I was startled, I was for the most part unfazed. After my frame was complete, I didn't just quietly appreciate the manifestation of my handiwork. I paraded it with unabashed pride and delight.

But this wouldn't be the catalyst that would go on to shape much of my adolescence. The event that engineered my transition into palatable manhood arose not long after the incident with the pink frame. Still so young and quickly starting to understand the currency of social capital, I soon realised that I would need to trade in the essence of who I was for the stability of a legitimate friend.

The sanitising and concurrent 'beefing up' of my perceived disposition would begin in Year 3. I was approaching eight years old and although I wasn't a loner, I had no go-to clique or group. I wanted a base of people to talk to about BBC's *Kerching*, *My Wife and Kids*, *Yu-Gi-Oh!* and the hottest artists out at the time. Finding kinship with a solid set of friends was becoming increasingly vital.

The universe eventually connected me with someone who would provide all these things and more. We'll call him Kenneth. We had been in the same class since reception but had never really spoken or had any extended interaction. Pretty strange, considering we were both Nigerian and lived literally minutes away from one another.

That small distance between our homes would eventually be the necessary channel aiding in the birth of our friendship. By chance, our parents would hire the same child-minder to drive us to and from school.

An enriching bond soon formed between us. Those journeys allowed him to provide me with an education I wasn't aware that I needed. It was during these car rides that my love for the sounds of R&B and hip hop via Choice FM began. I distinctly remember he had a particular affinity for Missy Elliott and Ludacris. Our newfound synergy, however, was nowhere to be found in the classroom or in the playground. Upon entering the school gates, it was almost as though we didn't know each other. It was back to business as usual. He would go to his nest, and I would go to mine.

Though I wasn't necessarily bullied, effeminophobia had me marked by everyone for not behaving like a 'real boy' does. I was marked by that pink frame and everything it supposedly said about where I fitted in on the continuum of masculinity.

One day, on the way back home, I asked Kenneth why we weren't hanging out together outside of our 20-minute car drives to and from school. To his credit, he did not lie or endeavour to spare my feelings. He simply stated that the way he presented and the way that I presented were at odds. He would go on to speak at length about the various activities and interests his assortment of friends had. A friendship group in which he was the de-facto leader, inferring that if I wanted to be brought into this fold, I too had to adopt these interests.

Thus it was simple. In order for us to be 'real friends' I would have to start acting like them. Like a 'real boy' or whatever that meant. I willingly accepted his conditions and rose to the occasion. As I was genuinely relishing our budding friendship, it wasn't hard for me to rationalise this as a reasonable trade-off.

And just like that, the consummation of my cleansing began. I remember immediately clearing my room. Ridding it of any ties to femininity, including the controversial pink frame. Reprogramming my brain to view both it and the mind-set that created it as sordid and inappropriate. As far as I was concerned, such behaviours were detrimental to my social mobility. They were a hindrance that needed to be nipped in the bud. Immediately.

Suddenly, I found myself pretending to find joy in not only watching football and cricket but also partaking in it at lunchtime. The other boys in my class were initially hesitant about my sudden desire to be involved in the sport but soon they acquiesced. I guess in their eyes, I had finally grown out of my confused state and become one of the guys. Sports being one of the definitive forms of masculine performance, my participation in this homosocial activity was welcomed with open arms.

A similar reception would also be present at home with my family. As the youngest of three boys, I was accustomed to my siblings regularly vocalising their aversion to my actions and interests. Meanwhile my parents oddly encouraged and, in some ways, nurtured the ways I was blatantly violating gendered lines. Considering the rigid ways African men are reared from a young age, it was quite remarkable that I was left to just be. My innocence and curiosities were not interfered with nor were they probed.

Towards the end of primary school, I had a wider pool of friends and it would be around this time that I would adopt a very conscious preference for the colour blue. Quite telling of the extent I had allowed the fierce indoctrinations levied on me to regulate my behaviour.

Underscoring more than just a mere change in the colours I began to champion, it signalled a thorough and holistic metamorphosis of self. This contrived and carefully curated transition from pink to blue represented a coded rebirth, in which feminine-leaning conduct was out and masculine behaviours were in.

Around this time, I was also starting to develop a reverence for my Blackness. Spurred on by myself and another friend of mine spending more time with the neighbouring class in my year. A class that notably had more Black people than mine.

I vividly remember a girl in that class known for making

cutting jokes about white people. Roasting their sense of humour, their cuisine and how culturally inferior she deemed them in comparison to Black people. Pretty fascinating, considering how young we were and the fact that we inhabited a school populated by mainly white people. Despite how hard she would go in with her roasting, her wit was embraced. Something about her comments filled me not only with great intrigue but also rapture. It would be one of the first times where it was highlighted to me that there was a natural magnetism Black people possessed.

I would become more attuned to this when I would see a group of girls bring in their CDs on a Friday. Making up remarkably impressive dance routines to the songs of 3LW, Big Brovaz and The Black Eyed Peas, displaying a flair and confidence well beyond their years, it had a je ne sais quoi that was sorely lacking in the routines the girls in my class were choreographing to Atomic Kitten, S Club 7 and Las Ketchup.

Conversely, I also distinctly recall moments where Blackness appeared dangerous, almost to the point of pathology. Prone to verbal lashings by white teachers, driven by their fear of the unknown. Rattled by the way the black children in their classes were simply living. There would be an incident where a girl suffered intense scolding as a result of the long luxurious braids she had done over the weekend with gold highlights. A recklessly ignorant statement to the effect of 'this is a school, not Las Vegas' would be expressed to her. Yet, at a tender 10 or 11 years old, this girl didn't back down. Audaciously defending her choice to style her hair the way she saw fit. Her astute poise and self-assurance was a fascinating sight to behold.

The latter end of my primary school experience was coloured by observing the radiance and luminosity of my fellow Black students. I learnt that being Black was simply the shit. I now wonder, whether my infantile steps into Black consciousness would have been realised if I was still the boy who initially yielded confused and perplexing stares from my classmates, in the wake of the pink frame debacle.

My masculinity was by no means consciously racialized back then, but I certainly had a linear idea of how Black boys were expected to behave. At the time, I didn't really understand what it meant to act and present the way I did during the 'pink phase' of my life. Years later, I can now see that I was seizing a level of boldness that not only would elude me for a number of years, but one that continues to elude copious amounts of Black men the world over.

Nonetheless, as convincing as I thought I was, as legitimate as I felt my revamped persona was, the little boy who decided to paint his frame pink followed me everywhere. Everyone could see it. Going to an all-boys secondary school, perceived threats to heteronormativity were easier to receive.

It might have been more tolerable by secondary school but my very presence unsettled the status quo of masculinity. But more specifically, it unsettled other Black boys' perception of their own masculinity. Meaning I was frequently subject to implicit and explicit castigation. Both in jest and in provocation. Sadly, this would be primarily at the hands of other Black boys.

Such experiences would continue to be mirrored in university. As with most British universities, the African Caribbean Society (ACS) was depicted as the site to forge friendships with other Black students on campus. I soon realised that the ACS only endorsed, and in some cases deified, very monolithic ideas of Blackness, especially when it came to Black men.

I, by and large, did not identify with the hyper-masculine ethos that pervaded my ACS. I found that I did not fit in with their overwhelming penchant to affirm their manhood by relaying hedonistic stories about their endless sexual conquests. This rabid air of competitiveness between them when it came to their virility and sexual prowess did nothing but emanate feelings of inadequacy.

Despite Blackness being the initial root of our connection, we didn't have much in common beyond that. My character ran counter to the homogenous Black masculinity in that cohort. But what was beautiful about that experience was that despite the challenges it came with, there was never vocal or outright disavowal of who I was. For the most part, I managed to have a largely pleasant and friendly relationship with most of the students who comprised my ACS.

University was where I was able to start embracing the core of my authentic self. Fostering loving friendships where the nurturing of one another's growth was paramount. As an English Literature student, my degree forced me to inhabit worlds that made me realise that I didn't need to live such a uniform life. Through the work of Katherine Mansfield, James Baldwin, Jackie Kay, Junot Diaz, Chris Abani, bell hooks and a plethora of others, I was able to begin dreaming and imagining a proudly dissonant path that I could fashion for myself.

All of this would lay the foundation for the restorative cleanse that had been waiting for me in the wake of persistent internal conflict and constraint. Unlearning and reconciling the traits that made me feel I was a black sheep as a child.

I needed to understand that what was supposedly 'wrong' with me was my strength. The issue was something bigger and far beyond me resulting in enforced suppression and preventing Black men worldwide from living fully and bountifully due to fear of ostracisation. Intrinsically tied to a shame we let suffocate us. It's no wonder why Black male suicide rates are so high.

I realised that this would be something I would have to

habitually combat by choosing personal freedom over fear. Recognising the power and boundlessness of who I innately am.

For the majority of my life up until this point, I let the colour pink and its presumed ties to femininity and queerness estrange me from a life of devout love for myself. Focusing on how the connotations of weakness and passivity clashed with a patriarchal masculinity. One that I naively thought would accept me and keep me safe. Failing to recognise that the cultural properties we've historically let be assigned to mere colours are ultimately arbitrary.

Nevertheless, pink is also said to represent love, nurturance, vulnerability and compassion. Why would those be qualities and attributes I or any other man would want to lobby against?

# Who Let The Dogs In?

## Okechukwu Nzelu

**I'M 17 YEARS OLD, STANDING ON THE DOORSTEP OF MY**
friend Ashton's house in Manchester. It's a Saturday afternoon and the plan (with me, there always has to be a plan) is
TV, tea and a natter. I don't have a lot of friends at this point,
so spending time outside of school with another person my
age who likes me is kind of a big deal. I chose my outfit with
care.

I ring the doorbell and wait. The neighbours aren't
looking, but I try to maintain a casual demeanour
nonetheless. I put my hands in my pockets, and then take
them out, and then in again. I cock my hip. There is pure
silence on the other side of the door. Then, out of nowhere,
I hear the sound of a dog barking. I freeze. Fear completely
takes over my body.

I have a fertile imagination. I envisage something at least
five feet tall. It prowls the premises, waiting to tear me limb
from limb. I can see it perfectly. It's got long hair and double
rows of slimy teeth, like an alien from a horror film. A vicious

attack dog whose breath still reeks of the last person it ate. It's a monster, just waiting to pounce upon the latest unsuspecting visitor to swallow whole and roll over for a treat. This dog's sole purpose in life, I know, is to devour warm human flesh. And it makes no difference that I'm here to see my friend or that I picked a cute t-shirt. To a bloodthirsty savage like this, armed burglars and well-dressed visitors are all the same.

I hear footsteps coming towards the door, but I wonder, what to do next? Should I make up an excuse or suggest another time to meet up, or just simply leg it? I frantically try to think of somewhere else we could go. Somewhere dog-unfriendly. Where I won't meet a horrific and untimely death. My mind is paralysed with fear.

Ashton appears at the door. 'Hi! Come in.' He hugs me, steps back and notices my discomfort. He looks at the dog, Cecile, who is now jumping up and down with excitement, her front paws comfortably on my legs. Cecile is a Labrador: every inch the merciless agent of terror I anticipated. I look into her beady eyes and see my untimely demise.

'Down, Cecile!' says Ashton. 'Sorry, I should have asked—are you okay with dogs?'

— — —

For as long as I can remember I have been nervous around dogs. Even though I've never been bitten by one, even though some of them perform nifty tricks, even though they are some of my dearest friends' dearest friends, I've always had a love-hate relationship with them. By which I mean that, up until very recently, I thought they all hated me and I'd really love it if they didn't.

It sounds like a minor shortcoming. Like not understanding the offside rule or having bad taste in music. But it's actually unpleasant to live with. Something that brings other people joy, comfort and companionship used to make me feel on edge. Every walk, every jog, every trip to the park was blighted with the possibility of what lurked around the corner.

Nowhere was safe. Shih Tzus would stalk me with bloodthirst glistening in their eyes. Pugs threatened to turn me into an evening meal. Golden retrievers tied up outside newsagents waited to golden-retrieve my entrails.

I think part of the problem was that I didn't grow up with dogs. I didn't even grow up with the idea of dogs as indoor pets. Much of my family came to England from Nigeria in the 1980s, where indoor pets aren't really a thing. In Nigeria, my family had animals, but only to perform specific household tasks.

My paternal grandparents, for example, kept a goat that ate much of the family's food waste. Although they didn't keep a guard dog, many of their neighbours did. Without a competent government to provide order and safety, people took it upon themselves to beef up their security in the face of a surge in armed robberies.

My maternal grandmother died before I could meet her but I was once told she kept a cat. It was strictly for pest patrol and it was never allowed in the house. Another relative used to take a hammer with him whenever he took his children to the park in his quiet, leafy, English suburb, in case they encountered any dangerous stray dogs.

'Why would you have an animal in your house?' a relative once asked me, genuinely confused. I didn't grow up with the idea of dogs as friendly companions so much as vicious guardians who were always on the lookout. As a child, I was once told never to run near a dog, because dogs think that people who run should be chased and attacked.

For many years, a dog was not a dog to me. It was all the things I'd been warned about, all the things I did not understand about this country. I was born here and this is my home but there are aspects of me that do not belong here. I am in this country but not wholly of it and there are aspects of England that I find strange and inscrutable; even, at times, frightening. It's not just the smell of wet dog. It's the class system, racial hierarchies, microaggressions. What's more British than the bulldog?

— — —

At Ashton's house, the question stands. 'Yeah I'm fine with dogs,' I mumble. This is clearly an unconvincing lie because he quickly offers to take Cecile out into the back garden and leave her there for the rest of the afternoon. My fear begins to wrestle with my guilt and my desire to be a polite guest. It doesn't seem fair that the dog—this carnivorous agent of chaos and weapon of human destruction—gets locked in the garden because I'm afraid. And I've been afraid my whole life. Isn't it time to change? This is her home, after all, just as much as this country is mine.

'No,' I say. 'Don't do that. I'll be fine once I've had a bit of time to get used to her.' I say and try to believe it.

We sit in his living room, eat biscuits, watch TV. Ashton talks about school. I focus on my breathing. Soon enough Cecile, oblivious to my anxiety, rolls over and exposes her belly. Confused, I look at Ash who smiles.

'She wants her belly rubbed!' he says, matter-of-factly, and stoops over to demonstrate. Cecile turns her head in ecstasy, her mouth wide open, her paws flexed like an old lady holding a clutch purse in the queue for the bus. This, apparently, is what bliss looks like. I laugh and give it a try, placing my hand carefully out of reach of her mouth. When Cecile doesn't tear off my fingers, I continue. This isn't so bad.

— — —

Over the past 15 years, I've become more comfortable around dogs; I would even consider getting one in the future. It's been a journey—a long walk, if you will—of self-discovery. I've never had a pet of my own so I've given myself a kind of exposure therapy via dogs that belong to the people in my life.

In my 20s, my friend Marthe had a Jack Russell terrier named Binker. I've since realised that Jack Russells have a bad reputation; apparently they're thought of as yappy little things with Napoleon complexes, but I didn't know that at the time. Back then, all I knew was that this dog was small enough not to present a major threat to my jugular vein. The average Jack Russell terrier is less than 40 cm tall, which makes them ideal sofa companions. More importantly, it meant I knew I could probably take Binker in a fight if push came to shove. 40 cm tall? I'm 182 cm, so I liked those odds.

Every time I went round to Marthe's house, I became a little bit less afraid that Binker would chew off my feet, and a little more comfortable around him. I grew acclimatised. I sat with Binker on the sofa, fed him, played with him, even took him for walks once or twice. Binker and I formed a kind of friendship. He had some first-rate qualities. When I stayed over at Marthe's house, he'd always trot into my room and say hello first thing in the morning. He was eminently cuddleable and good natured. He had absolutely no sense of personal space and I would go so far as to say he had a noble mien. There was something about that long nose. Even when he was sniffing a pile of shit, he did it with an air of respectability.

I think my favourite thing about Binker was that he seemed to have absolutely no idea that he was in fact an adorable little dog. Like all small dogs, he maintained an idea of himself that was infinitely grander than the truth. Sure, he ate out of a bowl on the kitchen floor and he could fit in the average handbag—but in his mind, he was the fiercest creature that ever lived. He guarded his territory ferociously, taking upon his diminutive shoulders the heavy responsibility of protecting the humans in his care against the postman. Truly, we did not deserve him.

A few years ago, when Binker died (of old age, not from fighting me), I was genuinely saddened, and this surprised me. Before then, I'd never really understood why people got upset when their pets died. Sure, it was sad, but animals aren't people, so what was the big deal? But when Binker died, I understood. Binker wasn't a person, but he offered a kind of companionship that was there one day, and gone the next. That will always hurt.

— — —

There's a new dog in my life now. Her name is Willow. She is my partner's dog, an Airedale Terrier, and she is unlike any other dog I've ever met. I'm told that Airedales are 'independent, spirited and keen'. In practice, this means Willow does more or less exactly what she wants, is almost inexhaustible and has an incurable obsession with squirrels.

Willow is also unusual in that she dislikes most human contact. Every other dog I've come to love understands that patting the seat next to you is an invitation to join you for a cuddle and they run at the chance. Willow, however, will look at the seat next to you for a moment and then slowly turn away, looking deeply bored and slightly offended, like a queen who's been offered some leftover chicken.

It's a sign of my love of dogs that I've come to deeply appreciate Willow without wanting her to be something else, or being afraid that she will become something scarier. Airedales were originally bred as working dogs on farms, so they were never intended to be reliant on human company. While other dogs show their affection through cuddles and staying close, Willow will happily wander off for long moments at a time and prefers to show affection through play. Willow's game of choice is tug-of-war. A couple of times a day, she will bring me her favourite toy (a stuffed toy snake: 'Snakey-snakes', to you and me), and we'll play tug of war until she tires of me and seeks some other form of entertainment, or smells food.

I understand now why dogs are so popular as pets. Like anything else that requires us to show care, dogs give us the best of ourselves. With them, we are patient and giving, we are active and vital, we put on silly voices and spend our time. How strange, and how fortunate that what once seemed so vicious can in fact reveal the things about myself I like the most.

I have grown up in a very different place from my parents, and my family comes from a place that is not really my home. Tomorrow, there will be new battles to wage, new fears to conquer. There are plenty of things I am right to be wary of, plenty of monsters that are all too real and must be fought. Perhaps that is why I am grateful that, every so often, the creature turns out to be an animal, the demon rolls over and exposes its soft belly, and opens its mouth not to devour, but to smile.

# King Kele

## Christian Adofo

**THE YEAR IS 2005. IT'S LATE AUTUMN IN LONDON AND** crispy brown leaves spray the ground like something out of an American rom-com. Glittering post-summer confetti. The seasonal influx of horse chestnuts are everywhere, ripe and ready for games of conkers in the playground. Or to quite simply lob/throw at other kids. Typical of what young pubescent males love to do. Tom—the original beg friend—is no longer in my Top 8 friends on Myspace. After a long summer spent in Las Vegas (I've got extended family there before you make assumptions as to what a 16 year old would be doing in Sin City), I was finally moving toward adulthood and taking my own steps to being independent whilst also trying not to forget my childhood.

It's Monday. 9am and I'm late for school (for once!) I hop on the first bus I see. As I walk up to the top deck, I'm greeted with the same old faces—my fellow youngers who couldn't wake up on time. The 'can't be asked' look all over their faces. Detention. Is. Inevitable. Some had scrapped school altogether, others were enterprising, hopping off a couple stops earlier to rescue day-old boxes of Krispy Kremes to sell at their own undercover tuck shops in the playground. After a few stops, a group of olders roll on the bus and everyone's demeanour changes. Fun facial expressions transformed to the forlorn. Scraps ensue over seats at the front a la musical chairs. They walk up to the top deck and directly to us, swinging their arms wide to the side, with their body leaning in the opposite direction. Moving in unison like a jumbo pack of K.A. Moments later, a few of them crowd around one of the youngers. He had just started Year 8. A witch hunt had begun.

The elder picked him up from his Just Do It bag.

'Townie or Grunger?' the older asked.

'Townie!' the young boy replied back, with confidence.

An older came up to Tom and asked him the same question. He replied with the same amount of confidence and certainty, careful not to give them any reason to question his answer.

I was perplexed. It was the first time I heard these terms. Apparently, if you were a Townie, you more than likely listened to UK garage and emerging grime, wore fresh 110's as well as oversized Akademiks or Nike tracksuits with New Era caps. On the other hand, being a Grunger was tied with listening to Grunge and Heavy Metal. The clothing aesthetic was pretty much dark in colour with baggy black jeans, sweatbands and rock band merch t-shirts swearing your sonic allegiance more openly.

It was now my turn. The older swung his head towards me and we locked eyes. He bowled over to me, with the rest of the group following. All bopping intently with a menacing walk. Shadows forming on what was once a beautiful day. I knew they were looking for blood. Looking for someone to humiliate. North London was awash with grime kids, but to be a Grunger was to be in exile. It was a witch hunt and the olders were the judge, jury and executioner. State versus Christian Adofo. There was no evidence. No need to tamper with evidence, cross-examine witnesses, conduct forensic examinations. Justice in their eyes was held by one statement—my statement. I stood on the dock.

'Are you a Townie or Grunger?' he asked.

He looked around menacingly. Everyone else looked terrified. I held my breath. The whole top deck was silent. No one said anything except for Tom, whispering something in my ear. He kicked me.

'Don't tell them the truth, bro'.

'Townie, obviously!'.

The crowd that had formed on the top deck went wild. I lived to see another day and original beg friend Tom had moved up the ranks on Myspace.

In my home, I had experienced many joys but it was my love for music that seemed unflinching. Music teleported me away from the immediacy of my six-storey estate view. It was the tool that allowed me to alter my universe, to step out of this world and move into my own private place. My own utopia. But now and again, I would step back into reality and be reminded of my North London life. My bedroom provided a bird's eye view of the ends, where you could peer down on the hectic warfare of TFL (Transport For London), where yellow sign boards from the police called out for information on misdemeanours. Grime and road rap was the soundtrack to the streets, bubbling up on mixtapes, burnt DVDs and pirate radio sets. The city was aflame with the sound of this music. Poetic lyricism bolstered with fire instrumentals, designed to travel out of our speakers and tantalise the minds of the youth. But rather than indulging in the music of D Double E or JME, I had my own obsessions.

The ritual of getting up early to revise for my A-Levels was routinely preceded by searching the Billboard Charts. Bubbling bangers that would blast through UK airwaves in the summer ahead. Patiently downloading songs on a sloth like dial-up connection from Limewire and Kazaa into intricate playlists on iTunes. This recalled earlier memories of recording chart shows on commercial radio just before the host would start talking and stitching together my own literal mixtapes through the family Hi-Fi system.

Whilst everyone was listening to the music that galvanised the streets, indie rock music had polarised my world. A lo-fi, less polished sound than rock, with lyrics that were either cathartic or chaotic. Indie rock music would be the complete antithesis to the sounds of the underground that were yet to crossover. Less raw but equally as rampant. Most lead singers were young white males who would come alive howling down the mic at gigs, stage diving into sweaty crowds with those momentary lapses of adolescence leading into young adulthood.

One day, I told my parents I was headed south to Brixton for a gig. The mention of the destination sent their internal alarm bells ringing.

'What gig?' my mum sarcastically said in Twi.

My dad chose to remind me of my 'upcoming' exams despite the fact that it was the start of the new school year.

I ignored their coded warnings and bopped to Finsbury Park, headed south on the Victoria line to watch the indie rock band, Bloc Party, at the Brixton Academy—my first ever live music experience. My mates were pre-drinking but with my curfew and perpetual fear of running into relatives I was on my best behaviour. Dressed in a dodgy caramel cord shirt (large up Lidl's fresh drop Thursdays), bootcuts and a wool Kangol hat, you could not tell me I was not the best dressed of the night.

The steep steps of Brixton Tube Station were peppered with people. Upon exiting the station, the exit revealed a mix of Rastas drumming, middle class gig goers waiting for mates to sober up and wide boy Cockneys turned touts, patrolling the pavement barking 'Buy and Sell Tickets!'

After some swivels, turns and a lot of walking I had arrived at my destination. I walked through the cowboy-esque swing doors. The air at the venue was different to the streets of Brixton. The heady concoction of dodgy hot dogs mixed with incense was no more. Instead the scent of eau de cheap cigs pervaded the space.

To be at a concert gave me a feeling I couldn't really explain. There was nothing that truly compared to this very moment. No introduction or anecdotes from my mates could have prepared me for what was to come. Thousands of people had found themselves in this one single building, eager and prepared to sing their heart out to the songs we'd all fallen in love with. Thousands of people had pledged their allegiance to the band, like they had entered a cult. Sweat fell from my eyebrow as I squeezed to the front of the crowd using the repeated refrain, 'sorry, excuse me', anticipating the start of the gig.

I was wide-eyed at the size of the crowd and the deep descent toward the front railings separating me from the stage. The pre-match warm-up riddim 'Kernkraft 400' by Zombie Nation provided a darts crowd singalong atmosphere where no one needed to know the words to the song and no one pretended to either. Instruments were substituted for ad-libs with clenched fist pumps held up in the air as the crowd bops in failed unison. Bodies flailing around, moving off beat.

As the song reached its climax, the venue was immediately cloaked in darkness. It was time for the main attraction. I held my breath in excitement. Anticipation grew more and more as we waited for Bloc Party's arrival. Rather through silence, it was channelled by Mexican waves and the unwanted fling of warm pints of piss trying to diffuse the obvious excitement in grotesque fashion.

The lead singer of Bloc Party, Kele, appeared as though by magic. He adjusted the mic stand and uttered an awkward but welcome hello. The venue erupted and transformed into a pressure cooker threatening to boil over. In Kele, I was watching someone like myself who shared the same commonalities. Born Rowland Kelechukwu Okereke, he too was of West African heritage. Although born in Liverpool, he was raised in London, like myself. I couldn't help but think about his own childhood. How he probably had his own utopia that he made, specifically for his music, a place that he too called home. How he probably listened to music to also get away from the trappings of his own reality, like I did. He had uniquely positioned himself in a world, which seemed so left of centre, so incredibly different and otherworldly. But strangely a place I could connect to when listening to his music whilst being idle in my bedroom.

The familiar riff of the band's single 'So Here We Are' sent me into overdrive and led to the first of many mosh pits that evening. Yet, even in the chaos of the sweat and mosh pits, I remained enamoured with the band and the frontman on stage. The guitar work. The energy. Kele's voice. It was simply sublime. Their humility and effortlessness made me stand up tall and not feel weird for liking 'headbanger music' as my Dad called it. Other memorable moments from the gig included Kele doing a Neo from *The Matrix* style dodge from a 1kg family pack of Dairy Milk that was flung toward his temple after singing the cult lyric 'he doesn't like chocolate' from their song 'Helicopter', one of the group's most well-known anthems to this day.

Kele was a unicorn. A Black rocker. A West African rocker. Performing to a crowd of mostly white men and me. Yet he appeared so himself and would grow into becoming more comfortable on stage. Kele's vulnerability as a songwriter and a performer gave me the strength to question the status quo and mould my opinions of a world I'd like to live in. Alongside my overt affection for Bloc Party came the fashion sense realised further with black Converse All Stars and a relentless sartorial appreciation for Fred Perry polo tops (owning close to every colour, akin to a pack of

Starburst) which allowed me to assimilate further into the subculture and feel less alone.

In the epoch of early to late 2000s, guitar rock music still had a stranglehold on the traditional live music sphere with only a few green shoots for Black artists at festivals such as Reading 2006 in my own experience. I vividly remember watching Dizzee Rascal headlining before rock band Primal Scream on the NME and Radio 1 Stage. It was brilliant.

The forthright rebellious energy of the Mercury Prize winning 'Boy In Da Corner' was infectious. Dizzee would confidently provide commentary on the realities of Black London life to a crowd of private school kids. This dichotomy was a reality that would only grow in the 2010's where Black British artists, namely rappers, would sell out shows to growing white crowds often from different worlds than their own. This meant that, whilst in 2005, the worlds of black and white kids were separate in some moments, by 2010 our worlds and experiences were well and truly submerged.

This required a careful balancing act for a person like me as I still wasn't completely away from the grip of popular culture. The continual code switching via speech and residential area left me feeling like a real version of Posh Kenneth played by Daniel Kaluuya in *Skins*. On demand enquiries at house parties from nervous guests on whether I preferred Biggie or Tupac. Others proceeded to raise their voices in the space along with awkward welcomes as they went for a fist bump (spud) and I responded with a handshake ready for an impromptu game of Rock, Paper, Scissors. I was in a weird middle ground during those coming of age years and this is an experience encapsulated in the lyrics of Earl Sweatshirt on his song 'Chum' when he rhymed, 'too black for the white kids and too white for the blacks.'

The fundamental truth was that I was, of course, as Black as any other Black person. Back then, however, notions of Blackness had more rules attached to it and these rules had more rules and on it went. These rules, it is important to state, didn't always come from us but they were always *there*. They acted as subtle reminders of who we were meant to be. They were most present when you wanted to listen to *insert rock song* or attend a *insert concert* and also when you were at a school having music conversation or debates on popular culture.

Blackness being policed is sadly an age-old problem. We have all heard of phrases like *'you speak really well for a Black person'* or *'you aren't like the other Black people'* or even *'but you're not really Black.'* These kinds of interactions are not rare. Examples of this kind of policing can be found across popular culture and media. When Beyoncé released her *Lemonade* album, white media expressed shock that she was unapologetically expressing her Blackness. Why? Because prior to that album, they had deemed Beyoncé not *that* Black. So much so that *Saturday Night Live* released one of their better sketches, 'The Day Beyoncé Turned Black', poking fun at all the white people who had their world turned upside down at the songstress being a Black woman. The white shock throughout the sketch continues as the white people, to their horror, realise that other Black celebrities are indeed Black. The sketch conveys how white America polices and categorises Blackness, deeming certain Black people as Black due to them fitting in to their limiting perception of Blackness. One white character in the sketch states, 'well I know he is Black' in reference to a man who resembles a rapper, wearing a black cap, gold chain and puffy jacket. Whilst other white characters express shock that celebrities like Kerry Washington are Black.

Then we have the infamous 'Black Card'. The imaginary card that all Black folk are born with by definition of their race. This card comes with conditions, the main being that if said Black person does not act Black *enough* then the imaginary card shall be stripped for them and they will no longer be invited to the imaginary cookout. Use of the Black Card is usually found on social media and it is important for us to note that much of its use occurs when fellow Black people rightfully hold those within our community accountable to harmful actions or words against the Black community thus having their Black Card revoked. Back when I was frequenting my rock gigs in silence, however, I was also partaking in activities that would have deemed me worthy of having my Black Card revoked.

As Black people we are understandably protective over our community and identity, a natural by-product of our global experiences and history. So the suspicion that some within my community may feel when coming across Black people who appear to display tendencies that are outside of what we are *meant* to be can be understood, but it is important for us to remember that we deserve to be whatever we want to be.

In the case of the policing that comes from non-Black people, much like what happened in the case of Beyoncé's *Lemonade* release, these are rooted in perpetuating the harmful and negative stereotypes of Blackness that reinforce views that Black people are one dimensional.

Back then, in so far as losing my 'Black Card', I had one memorable close call. I was 15 years old and I had a friend; he was Black and of West African origin like me. Nigerian to be exact. Like me, this friend also liked *all* types of music, including what the mandem called 'white people music'. Like me he enjoyed 50 Cent just as much as he did Bloc Party. He was my brother in musical arms. This was the ye old days of the Discman era. For those of you who don't know what a Discman is, I can only describe it as a mini portable CD player equipped with headphones. If that description does not suffice, google it (I'm sure many of you will do so anyway).

So this friend of mine regularly brought his CD collection to school. They were in a wallet that housed over 30 brilliant albums. A far larger collection than mine. Though I related to his love of music, I could never relate to his desire to expose his diverse music collection to the school kids. I felt he should have guarded them, concealed them from the judgement and possible repercussions. One day, when the end of school bells rang, my concerns were proven to be correct. My friend's CD collection was aggressively pulled from his palms by a mob of students.

Each CD was carelessly flung one by one outside of the school gates. They would scrape across the concrete floors, some CDs even bouncing off the floor only to fall again and scrape even harder. The previously glorious CD collection, I was convinced would never be able to emit music again. For those of you who perhaps aren't too familiar with the age-old CD, it is a glossy disc that music is played from by inserting into a CD player. CDs are sensitive, with scratches and scrapes ruining the audio ability and quality.

Tragically, my friend's torment didn't end there. No, that was only the beginning. It was not enough that his carefully curated CD collection was destroyed and that it was done so in a publicly humiliating manner. No, his audacity to have a diverse music taste and not hide it had even more consequences. The week after the CD throwing saga, my friend would be mocked and dissed by students often in front of large audiences. Perhaps the worst part of it all was that he even bought back his ruined CD collection from the students who so horribly took them from him.

For me this was a harsh tale of what could happen when you dared to be fearless in your music taste. Following this incident, I took it upon myself to hide my own CD collection, often inside my school blazer and bag. I would never put myself in that position.

———

So let us go back to the late 2000s when I was running around to gigs and absorbing all the sounds the UK had to offer. This period would be a time where small musical changes would begin. Reading Festival, for example, would now include a Dance arena alongside the Lock Up Arena, an arena for arguably the most hardcore and heavy metal artists.

This Dance Arena would soon accommodate homegrown Black British artists of African descent such as Sway & Lethal Bizzle. Rapper Sway, born Derek Safo, was another figure I looked up to, wearing his Union Jack bandana and fusing Twi & Pidgin English in his lyrics. He seemed unapologetically proud of his Black Britishness. A trope we would later see years later in artists like Stormzy, also of Ghanaian heritage. Other notable Black artists whose music made me feel seen in the spaces where I otherwise would have felt invisible were; singer CocknBullKid, music producer Kwes, drummer Gary Powell of The Libertines and Dirty Pretty Things, rapper Nkechi Ka Egenamba aka Ninja of The GO! Team, and Dev Hynes (Blood Orange). These artists, all being Black, took up space in traditionally white arenas with sheer confidence. They helped a Black music lover like myself understand that I could, and also deserved to, be in whatever space I desired and had the right to do so apologetically. Whether that be at a rock show, a grime show or an afrobeats show.

Today, thanks to the artists mentioned, we have a diversely beautiful spread of Black British artists making music they want to make. Bending, twisting and mixing genres as they see fit. They aren't just performing at camping festivals in an early slot but are now even headlining revered events in the music calendar such as Glastonbury. The impact of this would not remain in the world of their fellow music creators, but would also trickle down to music fans like myself. It would give us the freedom to also listen to whomever we wanted to and not in secret! All of the artists mentioned showed me that my music playlist can shuffle through any music genre and should do so without judgement. We deserve to be free in our expression and what we like.

The likes of Kele, knowingly or not, resisted any notions of Blackness and Black music existing as a monolith. In turn it empowered me to feel comfortable with my own identity through the myriad songs and styles which I fell in love with. My music taste and expression still remains as diverse as ever. From psychedelic rock, to grime, to electro, to afrobeats to dubstep and more. Once upon a time, these genres existed in silos, but the more you listen, the more you look into our history, the idea of music and people existing separately seems outdated and flimsy. We should all feel comfortable to listen to our music with freedom, to build our own utopias, even if they are situated on the sixth floor of an estate in North London.

# Pellet Gun Boy

## Jeffrey Boakye

**WHEN YOU'RE GROWING UP AS A BLACK BOY IN A CITY LIKE**
London, no-one warns you when you're about to hit the big
milestone. That point at which, somewhere between the ages
of maybe 10 and 12, you enter into one of the most intense,
potentially turbulent phases of your life. There's no fanfare
and no overt change in your day-to-day existence but rest
assured: as a Black boy stepping into adolescence, you have
just transitioned into a rite of passage that will last years.

Dramatic I know, but that's how all the best stories start.
This one is no exception.

As is the case with any naive individual waddling through
life with an outsized rucksack and a school blazer almost
long enough to reach his knees, I didn't realise what kind of
danger I was in until it was too late.

I was making my way home from school in year 7, walking
with some friends, ruining my dinner with whatever sweets
I could afford from the local newsagent and generally being

an oblivious 11-year-old. Then suddenly, the skies darken and a group of boys who are taller, older and meaner than we are appear from seemingly nowhere. At this point, David Attenborough's husky, faltering voice starts to explain how *these bewildered, innocent, urban young are now in the cross-hairs of a predator they didn't even know existed. It's time, to run, hide, or in the case of one misguided young infant, talk back...*

In the words of Joseph Skepta Adenuga, that's not me. That misguided young infant was in fact one of my peers, also in year 7, who got mouthy and ended up getting mugged for his trainers in response. I panicked and sidled away with a few others, learning in real time how to make myself less than visible in order to avoid drawing attention to myself and becoming the next target, the next victim. Welcome to adolescence.

Now, I don't want to give the impression that being a Black boy in the city is all violent threat and urban decay, because that's clearly not the case. I went to school with hundreds of Black boys just like me, second- and third-generation African and Caribbean boys from various parts of London, and most of us weren't rudeboys (the colloquialism of choice back then for street-savvy badboys). Most of us were just ordinary, geeky kids trying to get home safely. But London is a big place, and as you grow, you become a participant in a game of street masculinity that you never signed up for.

As I grew up, lost my waddle and got a more appropriately-sized rucksack that made me look less like a Ninja Turtle, I gained a vigilance to the threat of Other Boys mistaking me for the badboy that I definitely wasn't. I learned how to navigate the streets without drawing attention to myself: where to sit on the bus and how to walk past groups of boys in a way that wouldn't turn me into prey. I learned where to avoid on the way home, developed an instinct for safe and unsafe shortcuts and familiarised myself with areas of London where I was welcome or not. I lived in Brixton and my school was in Battersea, so South West London generally felt like a safe zone. You wouldn't catch me venturing across the river at all, for fear of popping up in the wrong area and being asked that bone-chilling question: *Where are you from?*

London has always felt like a collection of interconnected sovereign states that I didn't have diplomatic immunity to travel between freely. East London might as well have been East Coast USA. The thought of North London was enough to give me a nosebleed. And the deep South East, like Peckham? It was just too terrifying to contemplate. Before gentrification ripped through the area, Peckham was notorious for street violence and malevolent gangs. I don't even know how true the rumours were, but they were potent enough to keep me away. Back in the day, you couldn't even get on a train there. If you got caught slipping, you'd have to risk a bus, or escape on foot.

Closer to home, I had no territorial allegiance to my estate, but realised aged 13 or so that I had never even ventured into the estate next door. I didn't know the boys that hung out there and they didn't know me, so it would be instant suspicion and potential conflict. It didn't help that I was woefully geeky, all glasses and uncool trainers and a pre-hipster sense of fashion that was definitely quirky, bordering on weird. On one occasion, I remember rollerblading (yes, I was a rollerblader) around my local area and skating into an unfamiliar estate by accident. A group of kids stopped what they were doing and started to approach, a few of them laughing at my trainers, haircut and choice of pastime, in that order. I skated away at uncatchable speeds and was left with a slightly raised heart rate and this anecdote.

Here's a list of other times I found myself in danger, just by being out and about:

- On my way home from the Notting Hill Carnival and being asked where I live by an older boy who asked me if I had any money. I fabricated a lie about meeting my uncle in five minutes and he went away.

- Playing basketball at a local court with one of my white friends who was staying over for a few nights. A group of boys came over to jack his chain but left us alone when one of them recognised me from the estate.

▪ Being out late in the West End with some friends after school (courtesy of the number 19 bus) and being surrounded by a larger group of boys. One of us gave up some money and I got a punch in the face, at which point a nearby girl screamed, 'he's wearing glasses, he's wearing glasses!' and everyone dispersed. Insert shrug emoji.

▪ Being out skating with two of my friends, at night, in an unfamiliar part of London and friend A telling me and friend B to 'duss this part' (which means to go really fast through without stopping or looking back), because there were groups of locals out there who would want to beat us up. I have no idea if this was true or not.

Writing about it now, it all feels faintly ridiculous. All these boys that I was wary of, Black boys like me, will now be in their late 30s or early 40s, just like me, with kids and mort-gages, just like me, reminiscing over what it was like growing up Black in London, just like me. Black boys who have become Black men. Just like me. If I see a fellow Black man now, I nod in respect, in acknowledgement of our collective journey. I celebrate their existence. The fears and suspicions of old have melted away, like the fictional monsters of infancy when you start to grow up. I know that it can go wrong for people. I know of a few people who got caught up in stupidness, random beef, carrying knives, things like that, but that's the minority. A couple at most. The other 99% of us just went to college and got jobs.

College. Sixth form. That was the second turning point, the transitional phase during which I started to come out of the Black boy gauntlet and grow into a maturity that would take me clean off the rudeboy risk list. I was about 17, so still very much a potential target, but my affiliates and lifestyle were so far from the street that I was all but immune. Almost.

I went to college in Wimbledon. Wimbledon College to be precise. Wimbledon College is a Catholic school with a smart dress code based in a leafy, affluent kind of locale. No one from my area went to college in Wimbledon so I got used to making the journey alone, commuting across London with office workers and enthusiastic early-bird tourists. Due to the aforementioned dress code (blazer, smart trousers, college tie, no trainers) I looked a bit like Carlton Banks from the *Fresh Prince of Bel Air*, only less rich. Every morning, I would jump on a bus to Vauxhall and catch a train to Wimbledon. There were no large groups of kids on that route, so my guard was always down and besides, I was 17 now. I'd grown past all that nonsense, surely. Or so I thought.

'Yo. *Come ere.*'

I hadn't even seen him. A boy, who looked about my age, standing just outside the ticket office. He had perfected that cool, rudeboy aloofness and had singled me out, out of all the rushing bodies.

'Gimme your travelcard.'

What? I was being jacked for my travelcard? Are you for real? He was. I was too surprised to be scared and I think I just said 'no'. That's when he lifted back his jacket and showed me what he was carrying. Now, I'm no firearms aficionado but I knew it wasn't a fully functioning handgun. I'd seen enough pellet guns during my school days to know that it was a replica, and a thin one at that. So I just blinked twice, drew my face into my chin, walked away and caught my train.

———

Cut to: 15—20 minutes later.

Jeffrey sits on a sparsely populated train carriage, headphones on, listening to a bootlegged cassette tape on his Walkman. He is gazing out of the window. He looks up and sees Pellet Gun Boy. Pellet Gun Boy is not alone. Pellet Gun Boy is flanked by three friends. The carriage is now empty and there is no obvious escape route for Jeffrey. Years of vigilance have been for nothing.

Pellet Gun Boy asks Jeffrey for his travelcard. Jeffrey looks at the three other boys. He senses threat and considers his options. He hands over his travelcard and gets a shove in the side of the head for his troubles.

Cut to: Later that evening.

Jeffrey is at home pacing the room. He has a complex knot of humiliation and anger running through him and he is thinking frantically over what to do. It's not the lost travelcard that's the issue. It's the shock of it, the sharp reminder that, aged 17, he's still all snared up in the potential threats of the street. He's still part of it, even though he was never part of it, even though he thought he'd gone past it.

Jeffrey's eye catches a stack of old travelcards he has kept since about 1992 for no reason other than he sometimes likes to collect things. He stops.

— — —

Cut to: The following morning.

Jeffrey is standing outside the ticket office at Vauxhall station. He has been there for the best part of an hour and a half. Waiting. He scans the concourse looking out for a boy about his age who has perfected that cool, rudeboy aloofness.

# Pellet Gun Boy

The station is getting busy. If he doesn't go soon, Jeffrey will be late for college. Jeffrey doesn't care.

Pellet Gun Boy appears. Jeffrey's heartbeat quickens but his nerves are steady. He advances. He's rehearsed this. He reaches into his pocket.

'Remember me?'

Pellet Gun Boy looks around, startled and momentarily confused. There is a flash of recognition but Jeffrey moves too swiftly for any words to be said. In one swift movement, he produces a thick stack of used travelcards and throws them into the Pellet Gun Boy's chest, exploding in a flutter of orange, green and white. Pellet Gun Boy is dumbstruck. Jeffrey turns and leaves to go catch his train.

*End.*

———

And that genuinely, really happened. That was my actual response to getting robbed for my travelcard. It was dramatic and theatrical and did the intended job of making me feel empowered again, less of a victim. And it was absolutely worth losing all of those highly collectible (I assume) London Transport antiques in the process.

Revisiting this episode again now as a fully-fledged adult, I'm struck by how dramatic the whole thing seems, and not just the travelcards to the chest moment either. Being a Black boy in the city has a cinematic quality that can easily be translated into a very unhelpful sensationalism. I'll explain. The media has an ongoing obsession with Black male adolescence, ready to cast age old stereotypes of Black boys running riot around the capital in a maelstrom of violence and crime. We've seen the headlines and had the moral panics, always pointing at an image of Black adolescence that is at once dangerous and uncontrollable. Those fictional monsters I talked about earlier are kept alive by media channels that habitually demonise Black masculinity, a decades' old habit. It's an overblown exaggeration of the real situation, which is far simpler and far less race-bound: that adolescents across the board find themselves skipping in and out of trouble on the road to maturity.

I've been a teacher since 2007, during which many of my classroom years were spent in London, and I saw these trends across every cohort. The difference for us Black boys, us Black men in waiting, is often a shared history of economic deprivation and proximity to a potentially dangerous minority. Historically, Black families in the UK are disproportionately poorer than their white, British counterparts. This comes with deprivation, inadequate housing, and often a social environment that can breed economic desperation. As is the case wherever in the world you find poverty, this can foster and encourage criminality among that small percentage who are susceptible to such pressures. And of course, there is the internalisation of negative stereotypes that can further encourage impressionable minds to act in a certain way, like carrying pellet guns around and mugging Carlton Banks cosplayers for their train tickets.

I met Pellet Gun Boy again.

It was a few months later. I was on a bus heading to the West End, listening to my Walkman and, if I remember rightly, having a great day. I was upstairs, sitting near the middle of the bus just behind the stairwell, gazing out of the window and generally enjoying the view.

Without warning, a body slumps into the seat next to me, which any Londoner will tell you is deeply unsettling on an empty bus. I turn and there sits Pellet Gun Boy, this time wearing a pair of late 90s tinted shades. He looked like the third most talented member of a lesser known R&B band. He says something, but my music is too loud so I only see his mouth move. I remove the headphones and motion for him to repeat.

'Remember me?' he says, in a flat monotone. Being forced to repeat it has taken the intended gravitas out of the question.

I genuinely don't remember him at first, but my instinct is to pretend that I do, assuming it's an old friend. I'm telling you, I'm a natural born people pleaser of the highest order. So, in response, I smile.

'Hey, you!' I beam.

At this point, Pellet Gun Boy is so weirded out by the whole exchange that he immediately gets up and leaves. With that, I never see him again.

There's something profound in this epilogue that I'm finding hard to articulate. Full disclosure: I've been typing, deleting and retyping draft sentences for about eight minutes now, but nothing seems to stick. The general theme is around misunderstanding and discovery and the performance of a flawed masculinity. I also feel that in the sprawling youth club that is the city streets of London, any of us Black kids could have been friends, given time. Even Pellet Gun Boy.

This anthology is called *Mandem*. There's an affection to that particular collective pronoun that accompanies my memories of growing into adolescence. I hope Pellet Gun Boy is okay. I hope he grew up to be a successful Black man, one who I would nod at if we passed in the street. I hope he ends up reading this. Ultimately, I hope that all of us Black boys made it out the other side and can look back fondly at those moments we didn't quite understand at the time.

# The Audacity of Heartbreak

## Iggy London

**_TWO WEEKS._ IT TOOK ME TWO WEEKS TO REALISE THAT I** wasn't dying. I didn't know what was happening to me. I don't really get sick. I haven't had the flu in years. So you could imagine how confused I was when I was contemplating calling an ambulance to take me straight to the hospital and have doctors commence surgery on me right there and then. Naturally, I took the only civilised approach. I flipped open my laptop and went onto Google, searching for guidance on what I could be experiencing. It turned out my symptoms were fairly common. I was bed bound. I hadn't eaten in two days due to a lack of appetite. I had difficulty carrying out normal daily functions. I had this sharp, persistent pain at the centre of my chest and the only thing I seemed capable of doing was sleeping.

It's sad now that I think about it, but after a bunch of negative lateral flow tests and listening to Summer Walker on repeat all winter, I finally realised the cause of all my troubles. I was suffering from a classic case of heartbreak.

Have you ever woken up and your chest feels like it is fighting through cardiac arrest? You can't think straight. All of a sudden the songs that speak to you are the harmonious cries of R&B songstresses. Artists crying about how they were done wrong. You play songs on repeat. Again and again. Until you know every lyric, every chord change and every adlib.

I learned that there's actually a technical term for this— stress cardiomyopathy, a.k.a broken heart syndrome. I wouldn't wish it on my worst enemy. Someone should have sent me a memo. Spoke about it in the local news bulletin. Taught me about it in primary school. Anything to prepare me for this very moment. To give me some sort of reprieve from this unwanted agony that I was feeling. The government should have called a state of emergency when the first outbreak occurred. The first person to experience it should have alerted us to its severity. An epidemic—no, a pandemic! How it could take you out in one fell swoop and leave you feeling in a perpetual state of sorrow. How it could cause mind fogs, anxiety and loneliness. But there I was, in my single bedroom with a bucket beside me just in case I threw up and my phone opened up to an Instagram account I had been staring at for an hour. I was heartbreak's latest casualty.

It's safe to say that in 2021 I wasn't trying to be caught up in the raptures of love. Sorry Anita Baker. Hinge kept me busy. My weapon of choice. Oh, and by busy, I mean on a constant flow of dates. I had recently stopped linking someone that got way too attached for my liking and I was out on the town. I was known for that. Decent guy, Nigerian. Moderately funny, depending on who you'd ask. Too confident for his own good sometimes. I'd go out on these weird nights in Shoreditch or Soho with a couple of mates and I wouldn't talk much. Had everyone thinking I was some sort of mystery man from the movies. Fuck boy vibes some would say. I say flirtatiously strategic. Ducking and diving any form of commitment for fear of losing my youth. So once we were out of lockdown, it was obvious to me and to everyone that knew me that I wasn't going to settle down for anyone. Hot boy summer and that.

My profile was mad alluring obviously. It was deliberately curated. Carved out to be desirable to the masses. Black Casanova. Ex-poet. Five foot eleven-ish when I breathed in type brother. Dark chocolate complexion Lindt Excellence type brother. Spoke in a low voice, Forest Whittaker type brother. I would introduce myself with a hello and then a smize—a playful yet enchanting expression of the eyes. That would do the trick every damn time. Later that night, either at mine or theirs (I don't discriminate), we'd get our freak on—that 'boom boom shake the room' energy. After a couple rounds, we'd both be satisfied. But little did I know that this lifestyle of mine wouldn't last forever. One day I would actually meet someone, that would change all of this and would unearth things in me I didn't know were there.

When I think about it now I honestly laugh.

I arranged the date. Dalston at 6pm. Just thought it would be another one to add to the list. Bored out of my mind from staying indoors, a nice chat whilst eating Turkish food seemed like fun.

My soon-to-be ex walked down the stairs of the restaurant and towards the table I was sitting at. I was flabbergasted. 5'7, caramel complexion. Dreadlocks. Looked way better than their pictures. Like *way* better.

They walked into the room with an air of confidence and said…

'Hey Iggy, how are you?'

I didn't flipping know how I was. I mean, I had just laid eyes on perfection in human form. Let me get my thoughts together first! Blood rushing to my loins. A hit of pure dopamine at the slightest glance.

'I'm good. How are you doing?' I said.

'Good. Just going to run to the toilet quickly. I'll be right back.'

'Alright', I said.

What proceeded was something I didn't think could happen to *me*. The chemistry was chemistry-ing. Turns out my soon-to-be-ex liked musical theatre. They were a writer, like me. Caribbean, Jamaican specifically. Well travelled.

Spoke that good Queen's English. Loved all different types of food. We were celebrating their second alcoholic beverage since they quit a year ago. I gave it all I could give. The charm. The knowledge of wines. The conversation was flowing as much as the drinks. If I had it my way, I wouldn't have left at all. We would have stayed talking and drinking all night but the closing time didn't care about love at first sight. We stood outside of the restaurant, facing each other with our jackets in our hands.

'This was fun, we should do it again soon,' I said, chilled and mellow, but holding back the words, 'are you free tomorrow then?'

My tone calm. I got this. Instead, I said 'Yeah, I'll give you a shout next week or something.'

Despite my best act to appear unbothered, I knew the shoe was on the other foot. I wasn't in control. This encounter left me wanting more. I had feelings or something.

*Six months.* It took us six months to break up. Well, we weren't really together. And by break up, I mean I received a voice-note on a Monday morning from my soon-to-be-ex whilst they were on their way to a rehearsal. They had been out the night before and decided they wanted to be single. Crazy, right? My mate saw them grabbing up another guy in a club. Something about us not being on the same page. About not wanting to rush into things. I didn't know what to say.

When the voice-note ended, my mind instantly flashed back to all the times they introduced me to their friends. The times I drove them to perform at gigs and they kissed me just as they got out of my car. The drunken nights together. The heart emojis that we left each other before either of us laid our heads to go to bed at night. That deep stomach laughter we had when we thought the dumbest meme or TikTok was funny. I was confused because as far as I was concerned we were both on the same page. In fact, we wrote the damn book together.

The mind does a funny thing when you first experience heartbreak. It produces this highlight reel of all the best moments, usually in slow motion—so damn dramatic. So you find yourself laying down, remembering the smallest of things, from their smile, to how they walked or the tone of their voice when they call your name. This can last hours, days for some—but more often than not it can last for weeks, months and in some cases years!

Nothing could save me. Mayday, mayday, man down, man down!

*Four months.* It took me another four months to get over my ex. I realised that I was going through the final stages of heartbreak—acceptance. But by that time I had experienced all the things you go through when you are heartbroken.

Hope can be the biggest torturer. I didn't want to actually move on; to figure out life without them and have to deal with the reality of the situation. That my ex was always going to be my ex and there was nothing I could do about that fact. But sometimes we get so used to certain people being in our lives that we can't fathom living without.

It took me a while to get used to it. I usually ended things, now I was on the receiving end. But hey, sometimes, a good humbling is needed in life.

So take this as a formal announcement. Men go through heartbreak too. Even the ones with cold exteriors and dashing good looks. Everybody hurts. Underneath it we feel it, just like the women do.

After the break up I obsessed over changing my *look*. Yes that's right, we do it too. We are familiar with women post-breakups, getting piercings, tattoos, cutting and/dying their hair. The list goes on. Well, I started with growing out my hair. Before meeting my ex, I had short hair with shaved back and sides. Think Will Smith in *Fresh Prince of Bel Air*. I grew out the sides and leaned into my Kendrick Lamar phase. That 'I'm about to drop an album' look. I started hanging out in the gym. I learned to take my mind off the loss each time I carried those weights. I poured everything into my writing. Wrote more poetry for myself and finally finished this book. And for the first time in a long time, I remembered what life was like before it all happened. I'm not saying that feeling of loss completely goes away, I'm not there yet, but the self-work helped me forget about it a little.

In my sober state, looking back on it now, there were some rubbish moments during the six month stint. One step forward, three steps back kind of thing. One night, we would be at a gig, completely mesmerised by the band and each other. The next night we'd go about life as if we were strangers. I'm not saying I didn't have a part to play in it. I'm probably one of the most stubborn people you will ever meet. My way or the highway. I always have a point of view and am not afraid to speak on it. It's that Taurus energy. But somehow I wanted whatever 'this' was to work. So much so that I ignored the tough times because the great moments just feel so sweet.

My ex reached out a couple months later, after my grandmother passed.

'Hey'

'Yo'

'Did your grandma pass away'

'Yeah, two days ago. I feel a bit weird but it's okay. Hope you're good.'

'I'm sorry to hear this'

I'll be honest, despite all the self-work, a part of me wanted for us to go back to the good old days. To us staring at each other at that restaurant in Dalston, wondering where the attraction would take us. To us sharing dumb memes or drinking way too much wine for our own good. But I realised that it was just my mind trying to re-negotiate the reality of the situation. The hardest thing to accept about getting over someone is that in order to do so, you must forget about them as well. And so I did, I forgot about the times we shared and made new memories. Really great ones.

Before I met heartbreak, I felt invincible; a young man in London, living his best life and out of the clutches of a global epidemic. Perhaps as men, we are conditioned to believe our own lies about ourselves—that we aren't emotional and we can't fall for someone. So when we do, and it doesn't go to plan, we don't know how to handle it. It prevents us from learning our truth. I guess it is to avoid rejection perhaps. We are told that we don't need to be aware of our own emotions. Too busy to think about the possibility that everyone doesn't want to go to bed with us. Sometimes the lie is easier than the truth. Perhaps that is why I'm 28 and experiencing heartbreak for the first time. Guess I was running away from it the whole time.

We are taught that women are the ones who are perpetually heartbroken. That men don't have the feelings to understand their emotions—let alone be heartbroken.

Why do we believe these lies? Telling us things which

ill-prepare us for when life comes crashing down on us. It had to be anything else. An asthma attack or a stomach ulcer. But not a broken heart? That can't be it. You realise— after the second tub of ice cream, after sliding into the 14th person's Instagram to numb your feelings—that just as much as love is a feeling that can be felt by everyone, so is loss.

So to the person that broke my heart in 2021 by way of a casual voice-note. Thank you.

You made me realise more about myself than I knew. And also, why there are so many songs, films, paintings dedicated to being broken-hearted.

Of course, now I know for sure that I'm not going to die.

# Why I Wish I Was a Drill Artist

## Ashley Hickson-Lovence

**I'M IN THE FORD FOCUS, ON MY WAY TO TEACH A POETRY** workshop to Year 9 in a rural secondary school in Norfolk. Along the winding country lanes that take me there, I'm blaring out the song 'Crazy Year' by Dimzy, LD and 67. This has become a routine. A good drill song—blasted out at full volume—makes me feel fierce, energised, empowered. It makes me want to move. And at that exact moment, driving in through the school gates, I am ready, inspired even, to facilitate the use of similarly personal, playful and poetic language to the students I am about to teach.

One of my favourite poets, the American Frank O'Hara, didn't want to be a poet but a painter. In his 1957 poem 'Why I am Not a Painter', a title that half inspires the title of this essay, he writes:

*'I am not a painter, I am a poet.*
*Why? I think I would rather be*
*a painter, but I am not.'*

('Why I am Not a Painter', Frank O'Hara, 1957)

I empathise with O'Hara's words greatly. I am an author of two novels and currently teach creative writing in universities, but a secret I've kept hidden until now, is that I really wish I was a drill artist.

It's fair to say I've always had an eclectic taste in music, ranging from indie rock to Jamaican rocksteady. Raised by my St. Lucian-born Mum in our council flat in Hackney, I grew up largely listening to R&B, hip hop and soca at home but in my teens, my musical palate soon developed to encompass different sounds, with artists such as The Streets, Metronomy and Ghostpoet forming a few of my favourites.

Above all though, as a teenager and then into my 20s, garage and grime would become the sound that held a special place in my heart. And in time, as a new cultural phenomenon graced the streets of the UK, UK drill would become the genre I loved the most.

A Google search reveals that drill originated in America in 2010, with UK drill emerging a few years later, sometime between 2012 and 2014, rising to initial prominence in Brixton, South London. There is some debate about which collective in particular pioneered this new sub-genre, but from its early foundations, acts like Section Boyz (who then went on to be renamed Smoke Boys) and 67 soon established themselves as figureheads of this new, distinctly South London sound.

Since then, with growing popularity, a number of drill songs have entered the Official UK Singles Chart including Unknown T's 'Homerton B', DigDat's 'Air Force One' and Russ Millions and Tion Wayne's 'Keisha and Becky'. Most significantly, it was Russ and Tion Wayne's seminal 2021 single 'Body' that would become the first drill-inspired track to land the number 1 spot in UK Singles Chart, with the remix (featuring artists like ArrDee) later crowned the UK's most viewed music video on YouTube in 2021.

So, what is it exactly that I love about it? Firstly, there's a distinctive, somewhat juvenile rawness to the genre that makes it almost always infectiously addictive to listen to. Then there is the underground mystique that I find particularly alluring, exemplified by the (often, but not always) masked faces, the somewhat cryptic artists' names and the coded—often very figurative—language that I enjoy more than the commercialised, club-friendly sound of grime.

It only takes seconds into a drill track to appreciate the linguistic craft of the bars that are spat. In a single song, you will find more examples of witty wordplay and clever manipulation of the English language than in most other songs you are likely to hear in the charts. The typical drill tune tends to employ a litany of clever similes, which work concurrently to create a greater sense of relatability between artist and listener. Take these lines below from DigDat's 2020 single 'Ei8ht Mile' with Aitch:

> *'Talk like you're bad and you shoot like Kobe*
> *'Til you get left scarface like Tony*
> *Lyin', he weren't ever on like Iwobi*
> *I'm richer than all them opps, ask Sony (ask them)*
> *Still washin' up white like Persil*
> *Then I put it in a zip bag like Virgil (bag it)*
> *When I was on the wing like Ozil*
> *Bangin' my door like my house got burgled'*
>
> ('Ei8ht Mile', DigDat and Aitch, 2020)

It's undeniably skilful how drill artists like DigDat are able to cleverly incorporate similes that make reference to the film *Scarface* and household brands like 'Persil' to conjure the desired imagery for their targeted listenership by comparing thoughts, feelings and actions with names listeners are already likely to be familiar with. The lyrics highlight an admirable versatility of subject, theme and tone, and showcase one of many successful attempts to *include* the listener into the musical conservation, making them feel as though they are in on some kind of joke and not the subject of it.

As a huge football fan and former semi-professional

football referee, my ears prick up at the sound of a football reference in a drill song. But there's more to it than just dropping in a random footballer's name for the fun of it, there's real skill in the clever way these references are often employed. In Krept & Konan's 2016 single 'Go Down South' featuring Yungen, the football references humorously highlight the artists' portrayal as lotharios:

> *'And after my GIGGS they usually wanna party*
> *So I take em to the PARK and I get inside the NANI*
> *Or its back to the VILLA, she creaming already*
> *I'm far from XAVI but I leave the bed MESSI'*
> ('Go Down South', Krept & Konan feat. Yungen, 2016)

The playful manipulation of language above is employed to amuse the listeners; this light-hearted example demonstrates Konan's ability to employ puns for a particular comic effect, managing to masterfully reference a combination of Manchester United and Barcelona players over just a few lines.

The next extract taken from RV and Headie One's 2019 single 'Match Day', is an extended example with a similar impact:

> *'In the field we play foul, two boots up, that's a two footed tackle*

*I couldn't care about Lineker or*
*Jenas, it should be me and Rev on the panel*
*How many times did we score?*
*Excellent finish, should've seen the net, it just rattled*
*Shh done-done out Shh, fished him,*
*Should've seen his neck, it just splattered*
*Scored so much points from back in the*
*Day, we gotta come first on Match of the Day*
*All we did was attack like Robben*
*And Drogba, we didn't need no Makélélé*

('Match Day', RV x Headie One, 2019)

Here, the semantic field of football is employed with the inclusion of 'field', 'boots', 'net' and 'tackle' etc. However, rapper RV, as he so often does, adds another dimension to the clever complexity of the wordplay used with specific reference to 'Robben', 'Drogba' and 'Makélélé', all footballers who specifically played for Chelsea in the early 2010s. Furthermore, the reference to coming 'first' on *Match of the Day* implies that their actions within the song—which are ambiguous in nature—are worthy of opening the programme, an honour that is often bestowed to the best-performing team on the Saturday night football show. Essentially, Headie One and RV are top-of-the-league dons.

It's not just football allusions that make the lines of a

drill song clever of course. Below is a short excerpt from Digga D's 2020 'Daily Duppy':

> 'I got a dotty off one of my EastEnders but the son
> of a gun's not Nick
> The queen that I want ain't Vic but I still make
> that on the square like Mick'
>
> ('Daily Duppy—Part 1', Digga D, 2020)

The rhyme used, and the allusions to characters and places in *EastEnders* are undoubtedly incredibly witty and of course likely to heighten the sense of familiarity for the listener, especially for fans of the BBC soap.

As unusual as it might sound, since studying English as an A Level student, I have always enjoyed the process of close textual analysis, unpicking the syntactic make-up of lines of novels, poems and song lyrics. I started writing creatively myself while in sixth form and as a result of my study of Shakespeare in particular, I began writing sonnets aged 16 or so. There was something about this shorter poetic form made up of just 14 lines that appealed to me as a relatively reluctant reader at the time. I enjoyed the pace of the pieces, the strict structure and the condensed pithy narrative, which very often concluded with a thought-provoking volta (or twist) at the end.

Building on from writing sonnets, a couple of years after leaving university I started work on my debut novel *The 392*. Released in 2019 with OWN IT!, and set almost entirely on a London bus over just 36 minutes, *The 392* pays homage to the drill genre. In each line, I wanted to emulate the energetic pace and lilting cadence of a drill song by including linguistic features like alliteration, sibilance, repetition, rhyme and half-rhyme to help the words zip along the page.

In addition to how it is written stylistically, *The 392* makes regular reference to UK hip hop, grime and drill, as a deliberate ploy to subvert the perception that grime and drill is a genre that can only be enjoyed by young Black men. In the novel, the middle-aged politician character with wild blonde hair, Barney, who initially sits at the back of the bus, is seemingly ashamed of the fact that he likes grime and drill. As this extract below shows, taken from a chapter told from Barney's perspective, his desire to listen to a bit of drill is making him feel increasingly uneasy:

'It's ridiculous, isn't it? There's always the daily danger of accidentally blurting it out. It is my deepest and darkest secret; I can't let the press find out at the risk of tomorrow's papers reading: Barney is down with the kids but down with the voters. I don't want everyone knowing I cycle into Westminster listening to Kano or that I sing

Skengdo in the shower. It's a deep-rooted worry, but even now I'm desperate for my next fix: a smidgen of Stormzy; a dash of Dave; a sprinkling of Sneakbo. I'll even take the faint sound of a passing car blaring out some J Hus.'

(*The 392*, Ashley Hickson-Lovence, 2019)

Between 2013 and 2018, I worked as a secondary school English teacher, first in Tulse Hill and then in Cricklewood. I always felt incredibly privileged working in inner-London schools as it meant I was always around young Londoners and therefore remained relatively 'in the loop' with what young people in the city were listening to. While at the school in Tulse Hill, I regularly asked my sixth-form students to write down for me some of the songs they were listening to at the time. Not every suggestion was a drill track but many were and these musical recommendations catalysed my love of the fledgling genre. I didn't ask for these songs to ensure I remained 'down with the kids', I asked because I wanted to understand what pervading sounds were prominent amongst the young people I was teaching. I would quickly learn that for large swathes of young people in London, drill was the only voice they could relate to.

In the summer of 2018, I moved from London to Norwich to start my PhD in Creative Writing at the University of East Anglia. But every time I listen to drill, I am transported back to my home city, reliving visceral memories of growing up in my Hackney estate, and as I grew older, dancing in Visions nightclub in Dalston until six in the morning. Drill is the sound of London. In the backdrop somewhere, you can hear the cacophonous noise of traffic and sirens and crime and elation all amalgamated in a single song.

Drill can be infectious, compelling listeners to put up their trigger fingers, curl up their top lip and grimace in approval to the head-bopping beat. But to achieve this, production is key. As far as I'm concerned, names like M1 on the Beat, MK the Plug and Ghosty are musical geniuses. In a YouTube video he appeared in, uploaded by *FACTMagazine* in 2018, drill producer M1 on the Beat admitted that when he was younger he, 'played piano still, the grand piano...'

Even though the lyrical content can be perceived as problematic, over-violent or over-sexualised, somehow, the playfulness of the artist's delivery persists. Whether that be in the form of the choral sections—when more than one artist says a line or a word in unison—or interchanging bars between artists on a track (best exemplified in 'Under Surveillance' by Frosty featuring Unknown T and Headie One and RV's 2017 'Behind Barz' for Link Up TV).

Artists like Digga D, DigDat and Unknown T among many others can regularly be seen laughing and smiling while rapping in their videos, their arms flailing about energetically as they recite their lines vigorously. There is a joyous dynamism in the delivery that paradoxically subverts the perceived violence or drug dealing that make up the subject matter of the songs. Nutcase 22's video for his 2021 song 'Captain' epitomises just this and sees the rapper masked up and strutting around an estate alongside his boys dressed in a Mexican-style costume: pink shirt, green dungarees and a black sombrero. Clearly, drill is just as much about having fun as it is about violence; the lyrics below from Digga D's 2020 single 'Woi' show that drill doesn't always take itself so seriously:

> *'Stuck in the dock, hickory-dickory*
> *Fucked 'nuff gyal like Quagmire, lol, giggity-giggity*
> *Gyal wan' fuck pon Digga D'*
>
> ('Woi', Digga D, 2020)

There have been a number of public controversies surrounding drill and its apparent damaging influence on young people. In 2018, AM and Skengdo breached an injunction issued by the Metropolitan Police for perform-ing a prohibited song ('Attempted 1.0') in December 2018. The two 21-year-olds (as they were at the time) were both sentenced to nine months in prison (suspended for two years) for simply playing a song. This example, among many, highlights the overarching issue of some sections of society being unable to see beyond the aesthetics of young Black men (sometimes masked) making music to actually appreciate the quality of the songs themselves.

Drill is a genre that, in every sense, should be looked at more deeply than just at face-value. Even though the main themes of the genre appear to be about selling drugs, bloody disputes with rivals and spending profits on lavish purchases, a listener would benefit from seeing beyond the bravado to discover that drill is just as much about bonding with your brothers, making good music and having a good time while doing it. A large proportion of drill artists are young Black boys who, through their clever wordplay, are simply trying to get one over their rivals. It could be argued that this is similar to how football fans try to out-sing their rivals on the terraces on a match day.

In recent years, there have been numerous drill-based dances that have got the nation on their feet. These playful routines including Russ's 'Gun Lean' released in 2018 and Bis and MizOrMac's (from Harlem Spartans) 2016 'Mad About Bars', can regularly be seen attempted on social media sites like Instagram and TikTok from users of all ages. Despite the perceived violence and criminality associated with the genre, a quick scroll online clearly shows users of all ages, from all over the world, dancing along to music made by the very people they are all-too often advised to fear by the wider media.

For example, drill artists have been wearing masks

or covering their faces with scarves long before it became mandatory during the coronavirus pandemic. Is choosing to don a balaclava in your videos any different from rock stars like Kiss or Lordi or pop singer Sia deciding to cover their faces while on the stage? The mystique around drill is part of the charm, the masked faces are a performative addition to their costume. Drill culture's influence on wider society since its inception is undisputed; just like its musical sibling grime, it has reshaped how we use language and even the clothes we wear.

Undeniably, there's something strangely empowering about wearing a tracksuit, baseball cap and Air Forces, not to mention comfortable too. Kenny Allstar and Headie One's 2018 track 'Tracksuit Love' includes the line: 'I don't want a shirt that's Burberry, I want tracksuits.' A sentiment that many can empathise with, especially now that as a result of the coronavirus pandemic, and increased hours working from home, we have become accustomed to wearing our tracksuits more often (and maybe a baseball cap and trainers when we need to pop to the shop for milk).

'Ban Drill', a Krept & Konan single released in 2019, had a clear agenda to combat the weaponised prejudices that continue to surround the genre. And it goes without saying, that like any genre, there have been drill artists who have had run-ins with the law: Rapper Asco was convicted in 2019 for his involvement in running a 'county lines' drug route; Digga

D was imprisoned in 2019 for his role in a fight in West London; Loski was charged and sentenced for possession of a loaded gun in 2019 and Headie One was given six months for knife possession in 2020. These examples are in no way exhaustive.

It's impossible to disregard the fact that *some* drill artists have sketchy histories, but when you consider that a huge proportion of drill artists come from less-privileged backgrounds, you begin to understand a potential rationale that might start to explain the correlation between the genre and its supposed criminality. As you might expect, many drill artists grew up in areas that throughout the decades—through credit crunches, recessions and economic austerity—have been cripplingly underfunded and simply forgotten by politicians. Places where citizens have been pushed further and further into the margins, feeling more disillusioned and disenfranchised by the people in power, who seem to continually disregard the people lower down the social ladder.

Amelia Dimoldenberg, aka 'Chicken Shop Date' girl, has, for years, filmed faux-romantic interactions in chicken shops across London with drill artists from Digga D to Headie One. The success of her YouTube series is likely due to the fact that the videos have allowed viewers to see drill artists in a new light, one that differs from the swagger-laced depiction within their music videos. During their 'date', for roughly five minutes, we see drill artists sheepishly eat chicken nuggets and shyly slurp on their strawberry Mirindas while having awkward conversations with the comedic blonde. Their coyness is often surprising and illuminating.

Drill pioneer Headie One, who grew up in Tottenham's notorious Broadwater Farm Estate, is an artist whose roots are in drill but who is equally equipped with the versatile ability to dabble with different sounds. In 'Turn', with RV and featuring Unknown T, released in 2019, we are presented with Headie's traditionally unapologetic drill style, as evidenced in the lyric:

> *'I've been a bad breed since school*
> *In Citizenship, I'm trying to conceal this kitchen*
> *I'm trying to convince my teacher I'm a good citizen'*
>     ('Turn', RV x Headie One and Unknown T, 2019).

This is a section that rouses compassion, conjuring vivid imagery of a young Headie naively being sucked into a life of crime from a young age. In 2020, shortly after a short stint in prison, Headie teamed up with dance DJ Fred Again to create a refreshing eight-song mixtape called *GANG*. With collaboration from the likes of FKA twigs, Jamie xx and Sampha, *GANG* was a departure of sorts from the gritty drill sound that loyal Headie fans may be more accustomed to. On the whole, the EP varies significantly in sound to the music that helped him make his name, as does his full

2020 album *Edna*, named in honour of his late mother. The lead track from the album, 'Princess Cuts', has a far more polished pop-like, afro-fusion vibe than the raw grassroots sound we associate with Headie's earlier work.

Headie's success has undoubtedly paved the way for a wealth of up-and-coming talent. At just 19 years old, Bandokay—the son of the late Mark Duggan who was shot dead by the police in 2011—is certainly one to watch. As part of the collective OFB (Original Farm Boys), Bandokay's work often exposes an understandably deep-rooted distrust of the police, but despite the trauma of losing his father at such a young age, regularly demonstrates his versatility to weave between subject matters of varying poignancy. In October 2020, OFB released 'BLM' featuring Abra Cadabra, a song that masterfully samples Coldplay's 2000 track 'Trouble' with its widely-recognisable piano chords.

The track is a response to the murder of unarmed Black man George Floyd by a police officer in America. Filled with profound lines, the lyric: *'police on my back because I look like my pops/ Hold up, stop / 'Cause of that, why you want me locked?'* cuts particularly deep, as does: *'they'll see you in a group and call you a gang.'* Similar to the unjust treatment of AM and Skengdo by the authorities as aforementioned in this piece, it's seemingly not easy for drill artists, often young Black boys, to shake off being seen as the source of trouble by the police, even when—as we've come to understand in recent years—they should probably be looking closer to home for evidence of wrongdoing.

Frosty is another noteworthy talent, whose Daily Duppy videos for GRM Daily, especially 'County Lines 1' and 'County Lines 2', have garnered millions of views that could continue to catapult him to top-tier status once he is released from prison. The Country Dons, a collective from Farnborough, in Hampshire of all places, are also building a strong following. And not forgetting septuagenarian duo Pete and Bas, a pair of South London pensioners who continue to prove that you don't just have to be young and Black to be a revered drill rapper.

It's clear that with its infiltrations into the mainstream charts and radio station playlists, drill is here to stay. Canadian superstar Drake, perhaps UK drill's most famous fan, has featured on one or two tracks with prominent UK drill artists throughout the years, including his 2020 collaboration with Headie One in the 'Only You Freestyle'. It goes without saying that UK drill music is about more than groups of young balaclava-clad Black boys outside council flats making violent songs about selling drugs and stabbing people.

The content within these songs is evidence of musical storytelling; it's a form of cathartic social commentary centred on the lives of young people living in the fringes of our society. Drill is also a platform to voice a response about the trials and tribulations of 21st century life in the UK: stop-and-search, rising food bank usage, recession, Brexit, Covid, Boris Johnson's tumultuous spell as Prime Minister, the cost of living crisis, all of it.

Not to mention that the workrate of some of the afore-mentioned artists is staggering, releasing track after track within weeks of each other. The fast-release track culture of genres like grime and now drill has led to the creation of a resourceful communal sub-industry in the form of musical online platforms created by young Black men. From 'Fire in the Booth' to 'Mad About Bars' to 'Daily Duppy's', today there are a growing number of online platforms for talented wordsmiths to showcase their quick wit and their wily way with words. More than anything, drill is about the music, so shout out to K-Trap, Kwengface, Teeway, SL, M24, Central Cee and loads of others too for writing songs that almost certainly deserve more exposure and credit than they get.

Without doubt, there is more to drill than the suggested criminality. A listener must delve deeper to appreciate the beauty of the lyrics: the clever wordplay, the topical puns, the rhymes, and even more deeply than that, the nuanced notion of brotherhood during the toughest of times. The next step now is to entice more people from outside the usual listen-ership, like my rural Norfolk Year 9 class, to listen with an open ear and mind and appreciate one of the most brilliant genres of our time.

# Condomless Sex

## Phil Samba

THE YEAR WAS 2013. I WAS 22 OR 23 AND I HAD ONLY STARTED fucking a few months before. This was at a time when I wasn't living my best life as the independent, openly proud gay man I am today. I was still figuring everything out. I was for the most part trying to understand how to best navigate my sexuality since gaining the courage to finally act on it. So, I was making new friends, coming out to a couple of old ones and having lots and lots of sex.

I can't remember if I was bored or horny but one day I opened Grindr—a location-based dating app targeted at queer men and after some pointless conversations with imperfect strangers, I ended up receiving a message from this guy I was already seeing. We weren't serious or anything, we were very casual.

I still have a screenshot of his original profile with the old interface and the orangey-yellow banner across the top. His profile stats read: *27 years old. 6'0. Currently single. Looking for chats, dates and networking.* To this day, I've never understood what 'networking' means in the context of a dating app. Think about it—you're probably not going to make connections with anyone who will share your profession or industry, and you're probably not going to exchange ideas about your work. Anyway, his bio read: 'What's actually wrong with a simple "Hi" when chatting to someone you don't know?'

Basic rule of thumb, if a guy you've already had sex with sends you a message on Grindr, he probably wants to fuck again.

'Hi'

'Here we go,' I thought to myself.

'How are you?' he asked.

'Are you at home?' I asked back, skipping the pleasantries and getting straight to the point because, let's be honest, he didn't give a fuck about how I was doing.

'Yeah. Are you free now?' I told you he didn't care!

'I am. I'll come over.'

(I think) I left immediately after this conversation. He didn't live too far from me; I was living at my mum's flat in East London, and he lived alone in one of those newer buildings in South London which according to Google Maps is a 16-minute train ride away. I had quickly learned that sex with someone you're familiar with could be better than someone you're meeting for the first time. When you've been with someone for a while, you get to know each other's bodies really well, you learn how to turn each other on and how to make each other cum.

Whereas, with a stranger, it's almost like you're starting from square one unless they're really intuitive. It's like a puzzle you're solving together and that puzzle is your sexual satisfaction. Admittedly, I was excited about meeting him. I knew I was getting some; I had a good rapport with him, we got along well, and the sex was great. As I was making my way there, he sent me another text.

'Let's not use condoms.'

I remember pausing, literally stopping in my tracks, and being blown away by the sheer boldness of his statement. We had used condoms every other time, so I couldn't understand why this time was different. What changed? Did he not fear contracting HIV or other STIs? Did he regularly fuck other men without condoms too? I sent him a text that read 'I'm not doing that. I've never had sex without a condom, and I don't want to do that.'

Although he was really persistent at first he eventually respected what I wanted. I eventually got to his building; it was this stunning high-rise residential tower just past Greenwich. I had to ring his buzzer, which I hated because I always felt judged by the concierge. The guy answered and let me in. I tried my best not to acknowledge the concierge and walked swiftly. I got to the lift and went to his floor. I can't remember which one, but I remember it was quite high up.

His apartment was breathtaking. It was modern, spacious and the recipient of some incredible natural lighting across the living space. The man was living good. I mean his old place was nice, it was in Canary Wharf with stunning views but this! This we both agreed was an upgrade. When I got inside, I reiterated that the sex he wanted was not the sex I wanted.

'We're still going to use a condom.' I said, making sure my tone was assertive and clear.

'Okay.' He seemed a bit annoyed, but he understood or so I thought.

If I remember correctly, he was the one who initiated it. In fact, I think he always did. He kissed me passionately and I kissed him back. As I write this, I remember he was a great kisser. We were ripping each other's clothes off and made a small trail of clothes from his living room all the way to his bedroom. The kissing descended into foreplay; he got on his knees and he started sucking my dick,it felt amazing. After a few minutes of ecstasy, I pulled him up so I could kiss him again for a bit then I pushed him onto the bed.

'Bend over,' I instructed him, and he did as he was told.

I started eating his ass—licking him gently on the outside up and down, then swirling my tongue around before entering him, going deeper every time I did. He opened the bottom drawer of his bedside table and brought out a condom and a big bottle of lube. At this point I was still very weary of him, so I made sure I was the one to put the condom on. I made sure it was facing the right way. Then I remembered one of the few things I learned from sex education—pinch the tip of the condom before putting it on. I put on lube and he slowly sat on me.

'Do you want to take it off?'

'No!'

Suddenly, whilst he was on top of me and I was inside of him, he lifted himself up and took the condom off.

'What are you…?!'

Before I could finish what I was saying he was teasing my dick with his hole then he sat back down on it. I was shocked. I couldn't believe what happened and to be honest I couldn't believe how good and how different it felt to be inside of him without a barrier. His body felt so much more natural, more comfortable and moister than anyone else's had before. I really wanted to stop, but I didn't feel confident enough to stop it. I knew nothing about sexual assertiveness at the time—the ability to initiate consensual sex with a partner, express sexual satisfaction and refuse unwanted sex would be something I would learn later in life. Plus, everything felt so sensational, it was such a confusing experience.

When HIV first became known there were three things you could do to prevent it—use condoms correctly each and every single time, have absolutely no penetrative sex whatsoever or just not have sex at all. For over 30 years, queer men only ever knew two important rules about sex:

Sex with condoms = good

Sex without condoms = bad

Before this incident, I couldn't comprehend why some men preferred condomless sex but now, it made sense. I tried my very best to ignore the possible consequences of what we were doing. But post nut clarity is real! The distraction finished as soon as we both did, and now I was plagued with stress, anxiety, fear and guilt.

It is important to know that feelings of fear and guilt after sex was something I experienced often in the early days. The feelings would usually appear during sex or immediately after. It is the internalised shame that queer men hold when coming to terms with our sexuality. It becomes ingrained in us, affecting the way we interact with the world and people we're intimate with. The stigmatising conversations surrounding HIV only added to the shame. What is more is that it also supported and justified notions that we are not right. HIV is our unplanned pregnancy, *the* life-altering thing we want to avoid from condomless sex.

I used to worry about getting HIV, even when practising safer sex by using condoms, so you can only imagine how I was feeling knowing that I actually had condomless sex. I left the guy's apartment full of regret and fear. I had assumed

I was at extremely high risk of contracting HIV. Today, I know the risk was much lower because I was the penetrative partner, but back then I was worried. I thought I needed PEP (Post-Exposure Prophylaxis), a course of medication you take if you've been exposed to HIV during sex, e.g. if a condom wasn't used, broke or came off. The course lasts 28 days and needs to be started within 72 hours of being at risk; the sooner it begins the more likely it is to be effective. I knew it was available from sexual health clinics in the UK and could also be accessed over weekends and bank holidays from accident and emergency departments.

This happened on a weekend, so I went to the A&E at a local hospital. I was asked a few questions about the sex I had and who it was with. I thought it was important to be as honest as I could. The doctor explained the effects of PEP and I was tested for HIV there and then before being put on the course. Some people often stop taking PEP or miss doses due to side effects, but this stops the treatment from working as effectively. To have the best chance of success, every dose of PEP must be taken as prescribed. I finished the four-week course, spending the entire time constantly on edge. I went back to test for HIV and it came back negative, but it wasn't reassuring. I still had to test again 3 months later, thankfully that was negative.

According to the World Health Organisation, sexual health is:

'...a state of physical, emotional, mental, and social well-being in relation to sexuality; it is not merely the absence of disease, dysfunction or infirmity. Sexual health requires a positive and respectful approach to sexuality and sexual relationships, as well as the possibility of having pleasurable and safe sexual experiences, free of coercion, discrimination, and violence. For sexual health to be attained and maintained, the sexual rights of all persons must be respected, protected and fulfilled.'

It took me a long time to understand that there was so much more to sexual health than risk and not catching sexually transmitted infections. So this definition of sexual health is one that I hold dear.

I was born in the early 90s to first-generation Sierra Leonean parents in East London who moved here in the late 80s. I'm what you would call a proper 90's baby. A proper millennial. A proper West African. A proper Eastender. I was raised as a Catholic, was baptised, went to a Catholic primary school, did my first holy communion and later went to an all-boys Catholic secondary school where all my friends were straight guys. As a West African child, I was conditioned to believe that the most important thing in the world was what people thought of our family.

I was raised with the immovable belief that I must not bring shame onto the family name. I felt I had to put on a perfect show at all times. When there were guests, we would pretend to be a traditional, nuclear family to impress them. A lot of the time we barely knew who these people were, let alone liked them. In hindsight, I'm sure everyone could see the dysfunction. When we were around others, my older sister used to say it was time to play 'happy families' and boy did we play. This version of us wasn't real, but I was aware of the importance of this being the image the world had to see.

In my early teenage years, when I started to realise my sexuality, I knew it was something I couldn't speak about. I thought I'd lose my friends and I felt lonely enough as it was with them around. I knew that at home, there wasn't space for a Black gay son, it didn't reflect the image of the perfect child. To survive the mental turmoil, I distracted myself by pretending to be what people wanted me to be.

Section 28 was a law created by the Tory government in 1988 that prohibited the '…promotion of homosexuality' by local authorities. This censored and scared teachers and governors from mentioning, teaching or even acknowledging anything queer-related in schools, as it was illegal. This would in turn affect the sexual health information young people received. When the law was removed in 2003, I was 13 and really struggling to accept my sexuality.

What it means to be gay was still not discussed at all for

the remaining three years by teachers and never discussed positively by my peers. I even went through a period of praying, begging God to make me straight or at the very least bisexual so it would be easier to hide.

My sex education wasn't very inclusive—I was taught that sex was something that occurred between men and women, and that it led to pregnancy and if you wanted to avoid that then you should use a condom. That was it. This had me leaving school with exacerbated feelings of otherness. I had never been given information about same-sex relationships, sexual health clinics, or sexual consent. I know there are many queer people around my age and older who had similar experiences.

We were forced to navigate sexual health alone, teaching ourselves through friendships, relationships, and of course sex itself. On top of this, I didn't have examples of healthy queer relationships. Although there is a historic and powerful Black queer community in South London, I wasn't exposed to it as I grew up in East London. So not only did I feel like the only gay in the village but the only Black gay in the village.

By my late teenage years, pretending to be someone I wasn't began taking its toll on me. Praying wasn't enough. For the first and hopefully the only time in my life I started thinking about suicide. It seemed like one of the few ways that I could save my mum from the shame and embarrassment of being the woman with the gay son. Instead, she could be the woman whose son took his own life, which I thought was a better option in her eyes.

I was lucky to be able to start unpacking those feelings of shame in my early 20s. I gained the courage to come out to my sister, my nan and all my friends but coming out to my mum was the hardest. It was the first time in my life that I did anything that could bring real shame on our family. She begged and pleaded for me to tell her about my sexuality then immediately tried to shove me back in the closet when I did. Whilst I was ridding myself of the shame I had held for so long, she was drowning in it. I had no choice but to move out of the family home, into somewhere safer where I could express myself healthily.

I've been very lucky as my experiences within sexual health services have mostly been positive. However, I know this isn't always the case for Black queer men—many of my friends have had negative experiences in clinics whether it's been due to racism, homophobia or both. Whenever I've asked them if they made a complaint or asked for someone else to treat them the answer is always no. In general, Black people in the UK frequently have negative experiences within the healthcare system, rarely feeling empowered enough to ask questions about our healthcare and how it is delivered. Oftentimes, we are taken advantage of if we don't fight for better healthcare, which is why it's so important to incorporate culture within healthcare. Where would we even learn to be empowered to take control of our health to begin with?

Being Black, of African origin, and gay, I'm in three categories that are all disproportionately affected by HIV, which makes it especially important that I take care of my sexual health. It is part of why I wanted to start working in HIV and sexual health. This is very personal to me. We've come a very long way since the start of the HIV/AIDS epidemic. Today we have a multitude of prevention options, known as combination prevention. Combination prevention is a holistic approach where HIV prevention is not a single intervention (such as condom distribution), instead it is a mix of structural, behavioural and biomedical interventions, used to prevent the transmission and acquisition of HIV.

These interventions are PEP as I mentioned earlier, there's also using condoms, testing for HIV, getting diagnosed and starting HIV treatment as early as possible as people living with HIV on medication cannot pass on HIV even if condoms aren't used, so long as the pills are taken every single day. Lastly, there is PrEP, Pre-Exposure Prophylaxis, a pill you take before and after sex that stops you from getting HIV. It's the same type of pill taken by someone living with HIV to treat HIV.

Due to the combination of these prevention methods, the UK is seeing a sharp decline in HIV incidence. However, we don't see this same drop amongst all groups. HIV incidence in queer men in the UK is still far higher than any other group in the country. At the time of writing, whilst more than half of queer men diagnosed with HIV were white, more than a third were born outside of the UK. If you're a queer man and a migrant, the likelihood of being diagnosed with HIV is higher than any other group.

In the HIV and sexual health sector we are often told that people like *me* are hard to reach and engage, but the truth is there is no such thing as hard-to-reach communities, there are only hard-to-reach services. I want to reduce HIV incidence and prevalence amongst Black queer men by empowering them to take control of their health, expanding access to sexual health information, being open and honest about sex to encourage others to do the same. It is imperative our voices and experiences are heard in the sexual health sector, and that we are seen as multifaceted people who aren't reduced to stereotypes.

I've been taking PrEP since October 2017 and my mindset towards condomless sex has changed a lot as a result. There are many reasons why queer men might want to fuck without condoms. It could be to enjoy pleasure and intimacy more intensely or because they fear rejection for wanting to use condoms in a world where their self-esteem is often compromised by past incidents. Queer men are told they must wear a condom every single time which sets an unrealistic and impractical expectation.

Wrong condom sizes can be worn which can be uncomfortable, condoms can break or come off during sex. Some people are allergic to latex. Scenarios like these, can make men not want to use them. There's nothing wrong with condoms, but it's unreasonable and unfair to police and demand it of certain communities, specifically when they have lived with the fear and trauma of a heavily stigmatised, life-changing virus. Why do we as queer men HAVE to incorporate condoms in the sex we want? If a gay man chooses not to use condoms, why must he justify that? Typically, condomless sex is only acceptable for gay men in a monogamous relationship. This must change.

We deserve to have the freedom to be honest about the sex we are having, condomless sex is happening and always has been. We know much more about HIV medication; I can actively see the de-fetishising of 'bareback sex' because there's no life-threatening risk involved if you take adequate precautions. Some people hate the idea of PrEP because it normalises the sex, queer men have. Actively supporting the freedom for us to enjoy homosexual sex would mean agreeing that it's perfectly acceptable. I am tired of people who are not like me telling me what I should do with my sex life.

I hate being asked, 'why can't you just wear condoms?' We never ask straight people that. When they choose not to use a condom, they had sex. You might ask if a condom was used, and the guy might say 'she's on the pill' and then we say, 'not getting pregnant, then?' Like I said earlier, HIV is our unplanned pregnancy, the one life-changing thing we want to avoid. The choice not to use condoms is valid and should be supported as much as the choice to use one if said people are testing regularly. PrEP is relatively new; there's a lot of confusion about how it works and where to get it. We all know what condoms are, how they work, and where to get them. For some people, they are the best option, as they're cheap and can prevent other STIs from being transmitted.

It's extremely important that Black queer men teach themselves and others in our communities about the HIV prevention tools available today. Knowing about the many different forms of protection can finally put an end to high rates of HIV, poor sexual health, health inequalities and HIV stigma. Talking to our friends and partners openly about sexual health can not only improve our knowledge and wellbeing in connection to sex but can also have a positive impact on our sex lives. Motivating others to test and detect things early can make all the difference. HIV mirrors the inequalities in the world, but we must do our best to change this. It might take longer; it might be more difficult but we owe it to ourselves.

We deserve to have the sex *we* want. Sex that is healthy. Sex that is not harmful. Sex that is free. Sex that is pleasurable.

# How to Build an Immigrant

## Dipo Faloyin

HERE'S A FACT MASQUERADING AS A RIDDLE: THERE ARE many ways to pronounce my name, yet only one is correct.

On seeing it written down, you may be tempted to fix yourself to say '*DIP*' before rounding off with an '*OH*'. That is understandable. That is wrong. Perhaps, instead, on sight you reach for '*DIE*' followed by '*POH*'. That, too, is wrong— and, honestly, incongruent to think, let alone say.

The most common variation—what seems, for many, to be the most natural instinct—is to pronounce it '*DEE*' accompanied by a softened '*PO*'; lips puckered, set to rest. And though this is actually how I introduce myself to non-Nigerians, it is still wrong.

The correct pronunciation of my name actually starts with the aforementioned '*DEE*' then quickly smuggles in a shy '*K*' sound that effortlessly combines with a '*PAW*'—try it.

Muscle memory is all that's needed for a Nigerian tongue to wrap and form the sound on sight. There is a weightiness to it; a slight tug on the back of your tongue

**147**

that is unexpected. Non-native mouths experience several stumbles, a little skip and sliding jump before landing on the right beat.

I grew up in a place where everyone looked like me and, importantly, they had names like mine. Nigeria. This comfort, however, would not last. I was soon to enter into a new world at the tender age of 10—a country of people for whom my name would present itself as a barrier they had to scale when they'd rather not exert the required energy. In my name, in my being, there would be a weightiness to my existence. This place? The United Kingdom.

Even at such a young age I was able to comprehend the potential issues this could create. So, I decided, I didn't want people to stumble at the mere suggestion of my presence. I mean, who would. Something had to be done.

———

Reinventions are rare.

There are, maybe, a handful of times across a person's life where they find themselves living among a new community of potential friends, acquaintances, neighbours and enemies. You can, in these rare moments, reinvent yourself, and you can do so without worrying that somebody from your past will expose you. In this new world, no one can prove that you're not, in fact, cool or into indie music or particularly adventurous or speak in memes and like football. You are free to recreate the person you deem most appropriate for the new community you are living amongst.

Normally these landmarks occur when you change schools, or when you move to a new city. In my case it was both. I remember the conversation my parents had with me in Lagos. They called me up to their room and communicated in a gentle, yet assured tone.

'We're sending you to Bath,' they said.

'Where?' I replied.

After explaining the city was in the UK, I was pretty excited—it felt like a far greater adventure than I had ever imagined. At the time, I was months away from finishing primary school, and the plan, as far as I knew it, was for me to go to boarding school somewhere within the confines of Nigeria. But my parents had—as parents often do—made other arrangements without consulting me. Together they had decided to ship me on the proverbial boat from Lagos, the cultural heartbeat of Africa's most populous country and the Blackest city in the world, to somewhere that very much was not the Blackest city in the world.

— — —

Reinventions are rare.

And when you're Black, they can be very complicated.

With the excitement came an understanding that, for the first time in my life, I was about to be fundamentally different from everyone else around me. I would look different, sound different and to all who met me, my name would be a constant reminder of this. I understood that people would see me and immediately expect something from me—expect something from the fact that I was coming from this great expanse they only knew as Africa, with their visions of an unknowable landscape and wild dangers hiding in every bush. It was this pressure that turned my mind into immediately thinking about what I might need to change.

This was the late 90s. Years before afrobeats, zanku, peak Jay-Jay Okocha, Detty December and The Year of Return. It was not yet cool to be Nigerian. At the time, the idea of Black Britishness was largely a mystery to me and my friends in Lagos. Pop culture had told us that there was one universal recognition of Blackness: African American. A certain type of identity that for us, had been curated via American sitcoms, MTV and theories about who shot Biggie and Tupac. To be 'Internationally Black' in my young mind was to like *The Fresh Prince*, *Living Single*, *Moesha* and *Martin!* It was Boys II Men, 50 Cent and Snoop Dogg; it was BET, *TRL* and *106 & Park*.

Of course there was a lot more to Black American culture, but I was a 10 year old kid from Lagos and these were the things that traversed across the seas and to every corner and crevice of the world. This was why Nigerian artists back then were rapping in St. Louis accents. It was why I owned a white t-shirt four sizes too big for me. It was why my full name seemed like something worth abandoning for the convenience of others. The African version of Black culture was shrouded in misunderstanding and stigma. For many, 'Africaness' was limited to a few things—the poverty they saw in charity fundraisers, depictions of animals running wild and warriors hopping up and down. At 10 years old, I figured out that I could flatten my name, accent or even origin story and just like that, it could make my life that little bit easier.

Moving to the UK meant that I was actively searching for what it meant to be Black and British, and if I could fit within its confines.

What I settled on first was my name. I've always loved it, so it wasn't so much that it represented something that I actively wanted to give up. But as minority communities know too well, the understanding that my full self was negotiable was clear to me, especially, if it meant peace. I knew my name to be an inconvenience to others not well-versed in Nigerian monikers. My thinking was also made easier by having a middle name that was far more universal: Emmanuel. With my mind made, I decided to run the decision by my parents.

'I think it would be easier if I went by Emmanuel at school,' I said, more as an announcement than a request.

'You can, if you want,' they replied. 'But I think one day you will learn to value being different.'

There was a serenity to their tone that immediately put me at ease, happy to rest in their assuredness, I decided to go forth and become Emmanuel.

While I was concerned about my personal brand, it's safe to say my parents were very much not. They were preoccupied by something else: my safety. Looming over this move was the reality of a tragedy, one that today remains etched in the memory of the UK: the murder of Stephen Lawrence—a young man whose only crime to some was that he existed at all. Lawrence was killed while waiting for a bus in 1993, in a brutal, unprovoked attack.

Six years later, as I prepared to move to the UK, not a single one of his attackers had been convicted of the crime. It would take another decade for two men to be brought to trial and eventually sentenced. 'See how they just killed that boy,' I heard aunties and uncles say around our home. Discussing his death was not to scare me or put me off my new home. After all, they were the ones sending me to the UK in the hope that I would never become complacent. They wanted me to explore and, eventually if I stayed long enough, become a part of British society, as much as I could be.

Just a few months after arriving in the UK, another young Nigerian boy, almost the same age as me, was killed in Peckham, London. Damilola Taylor's family, as with the Lawrences, would wait years for justice, but never really find peace. It was this absence of peace that my parents feared most.

— — —

For many immigrants, by the time you're ready to move, you've spent most of your preparation pre-occupied by ways you can flatten yourself, not appearing too rigid, willing to be remoulded in an image that others will deem inoffensive. It's a lot for a 10-year-old to take on and it's something everyone should consider when you hear discussions play out publicly about forcing people to assimilate.

In many ways I was lucky. I had family in the UK— aunts, uncles, cousins and people you refer to as your aunt/ uncle/cousin who are not. I had roots to tangle up with. I had visited London several times on holiday—specifically Shepherd's Bush where I spent weeks crashing with my aunt and granny. The city was—and is—easy to love: diverse, compact, free, moveable. There is so much in so many corners, nestled gently next to each other.

London can be hard to navigate if you don't know where to look but Bath was a mystery to me. The weeks I spent in London before I moved to boarding school were filled with daily, psychological expeditions in search of a way of presenting myself effectively. I came to realise that the city is not just diverse in sight, but also in its people. There were many different ways to be different, each seemingly valued if you found the right clique.

I was now 11 years old living in Bath. As far as I knew, there were two types of *Immigrant* Black, this kind of Black differed from the cool, relatively accepted iteration of African American Blackness.

The categories of this type of Black were: 'Fresh Off the Boat' Black or the 'Child of Someone Who Was Fresh Off The Boat' Black. The latter was a Blackness formed from being kids of immigrants, born in the UK to parents of the diaspora. For us Nigerians, it meant you ate jollof at home, you understood pidgin and people smiled politely at your attempt to speak Yoruba; your parents threatened that they'd send you back home and though you took it as a threat, you were never certain what that would actually mean in reality. You danced delicately across lines of what it meant to be British, unsure if you even fitted in at times—yet much of Britain, or the city you lived in felt like home.

You were different enough and knew where you came from. If there wasn't a stigma around being seen as generically African, this experience would have felt like the best of both worlds, and would allow you to easily teleport between both worlds. I wished at the time I could do that. My challenge was complicated by the fact I sounded Nigerian, an immediate sign that maybe I was different. I was spoken to like I was different. In no way was I embarrassed of being Nigerian, but Africa's most populous country may not have been as pop culturally relevant as it is today, but it was then, as it is now, a special place. Yet I knew the challenges minority groups faced. I knew that in every interaction, I would be defined before I could even define myself.

So I muzzled myself the easiest way I knew how: I adapted the way I spoke. British accents are not the easiest to imitate, largely because until you move to the UK, you don't appreciate the variety of speaking patterns that exist. There was one resource in Lagos—*Eastenders*, a show that travelled across the seasons and nestled in the hearts of countless Nigerian parents and grandparents. The first time I tried a cockney accent was on a five-a-side football pitch in Shepherd's Bush during one of my early visits to the capital as a child. My cousin, who lived in London, stopped playing, turned to me and said firmly: 'never do that again,' and carried on playing.

———

Bath was very different to the diverse utopia of the capital, and certainly a million miles from Lagos. Bath is one of the most beautiful cities in the country. But as a young Black boy, when you hear that it's the sort of city that requires you to use a specific type of limestone on all new constructions, you begin to worry that maybe you're the wrong type of material for the city's foundations.

There are few discussions about what diversity means outside of diverse areas—closing off opportunities for minority communities to expand across the country because many people, understandably, feel like London and a handful of other cities—if that—are the only places that they will feel welcome. We focus our conversations around West Indian communities in Brixton and Asian neighbourhoods in Birmingham. The unspoken assumption is that minority communities should stick within cities that have a large, well-established concentration of their own. Large parts of this country, rightly or wrongly, are not under serious consideration as options to set up home. Many just don't feel safe outside of what they know.

Having options is a great luxury, especially as London is getting more and more expensive and seems determined to gentrify every last neighbourhood. For Black people to feel comfortable moving to more rural areas of the country, we need to collectively examine how welcoming these communities are to different types of limestone. We need to ask how many small towns and villages felt compelled to hold BLM rallies or put in place procedures to hold their own communities accountable for discriminatory policies. Life could be easier for Black and Brown communities in areas outside of these major cities that are growing more and more as playing grounds for a select few and money sucking devices for everyone else. You should be able to move out without worrying about your safety.

— — —

It's easy to fall in love with British politeness. My parents certainly did. Bath was everything many Nigerian parents look for when considering where to plant their children: traditional, clean, safe and stable in relation to the volatility of London. However my parents were not necessarily putting their faith in the city, but in another cocoon: boarding school. They knew it would not match the diversity of a city like London, but they trusted in my school's decency and the fact that it had a long history in playing host to international students.

My parents were confident that I would be safe, largely because that and a good education were exactly what they were paying for—a luxury that many people don't have. I was torn. The version of me that I was moulding was based on what London might expect from me. I had a strong sense of who I could be in a city full of Nigerians; a place fuelled by the idea of new people arriving every day.

My parents reminded me what an incredible experience this had the potential to be. But next to that were conversations about staying safe, and not forgetting that the rules that would govern me—a Black boy in a traditional British environment—would not always apply to my white friends. They wanted me to be comfortable, happy and trusting, but vigilant. These were the constant discussions my parents had with me. We spoke at length about how to navigate potentially harmful situations. My parents were excited for me and the opportunity being in a new environment would bring. Between the three of us, we had every side covered; they worried about my safety and I worried about how I was to attain social credibility.

Boarding school officially baptised me as an immigrant boy, it taught me the rules and lessons surrounding this new identity. For the first time in my life, when introducing myself to someone new, I had to think about any preconceptions that may have about what it meant to be from Nigeria.

In Nigeria, I wasn't an immigrant boy—I was just a boy. Now I was fielding questions about poverty in Africa and evil dictators.

This is how you build an immigrant boy—a procedure many minority families are all too familiar with. Not being able to present your full self at such a young age sits with you, and it doesn't shake off easily. You have to unlearn the made up belief that you are not enough. That your name is not beautiful or normal. That you have to be someone you are not just to fit into this idea of Britishness. The potential repercussions of this experience can be detrimental.

All the while, some people can just turn up and introduce themselves. Why? Because everyone knows how to pronounce the name Dave.

# Are You a Bowcat?

## Jordan Stephens

**HE PUT THE GUN IN MY FACE. WHICH IS OUT OF ORDER REALLY.**
Unwritten rule. Unless you really mean it or you're in a war
or something. You never playfully point a gun at anyone. It's
not funny. And yet here he is. Posing with a decommissioned
handgun. Using me to feel something.

I'm the youngest here. This is his bedroom. Big Hen.
That's what he's known as round here. He makes music.
Drags and drops. Never seen him play an instrument. The
room's small. He lives with his mum and grandmother.
There's a single window facing the street. The roof slants just
above it giving the room an attic feel. I'd put money on there
being skeletons. Single bed. Shit stuffed under it. Ashtrays
everywhere. Bits of weed. Teenage boy vibes. Old bowls and
loose socks. Enough places to sit though. People always
come here for a little drink and a shit story. Bring back home
some girls and try their chances. There's four of us here now.
Different spectrums of teenager. All idiots, really.

His little brother is bigger than him. They're both fucking

huge though. Fat and tall. 'Don't start on them' size. Let it go if he bumps into you at a club size. I can't figure out if they like me or not. I'm here after all. I've been let through the door. But my understanding of social cues is way off. Always has been. A lonely, wild only child. A little Black boy around rich white boy energy. I'll just go round asking people questions.

I'm suspiciously interested in people's lives. But once the hormones kicked in and everyone was fighting and hanging out in parks I didn't get it. I stayed inside and watched films. Taught myself graphic design. Felt like a more productive use of energy. Friendship seemed taxing. And before I knew it I was unsure how to identify what friendship even was. Or how to maintain it. But there was common ground with a couple of these boys. They make music. I make music. I wish I was cool like them. They don't mind me being there.

We're all crowding around a computer. That's the Sun. Centre of the universe. Big Hen's playing music off it. Got MSN messenger on in the background. 'Have you got a webcam?' and shit. 'Flash for us'. The goal is to have a girl put your name in their username. Ideally in between two stars. Not two hearts though, that'll scare other girls off. Just being listed in the name is good. I can't think of anything more validating right now than being included in someone's username on MSN. A social zenith. I'm part of the computer's gravitational pull but on the outskirts. I'm Neptune or Pluto.

A real-time depiction of my social status. And I've remained here. Even as Big Hen returned to his computer chair after 'showing me' his gun.

I'm unusually quiet because I don't know where I stand. Even with my cubic zirconia diamond earrings in both ears and my pink and brown converse. I don't feel confident. Hen trying to shoot me didn't help. Another of the gang, Dylan, starts making jokes. More of the same. Who had a fight the other night. Which girl is the most likely to fuck one of them. Dylan's lanky and mixed race like me. Best rapper about. Wicked sense of humour. A little crazy. He's got a good rapper face. When it's relaxed it looks menacing. Got a shady brow. I sometimes wonder if my face is too friendly to be a rapper. Strangers ask me for directions on the street.

Dylan turns his attention to me. He glances over and asks me a question.

'Yo, you a bowcat?'

On my life I don't know what that word means. The other boys have gone quiet. Awaiting my response. Giving away nothing. I wonder if it's a trick question. I try and use denomination to figure it out and get nowhere. I'm worried this'll fuck my standing in the group. A bowcat. We're talking about girls. Maybe they're asking if I'm a girl. Teasing me. I get the wrong end of the stick a lot. When I was in primary school this bully called me a 'gaylord' and I said, 'thank you'. Genuinely believing it was a compliment. He was baffled. It is a compliment in my eyes. I do say 'gay' nowadays when describing something shit though. It's just what people say. I just go along with it. Growing up is messy.

'Do you know what a bowcat is?'

I shake my head. Just a little bit. Quickly. Wincing almost. In preemption of laughter. It never comes.

'Do you lick girls out?'

'Oh, I think. Oh.'

I say. Feels like everyone's leaning in now. I have now become the Sun. They want the heat. Hanging on my every word. Silly question. Obvious answer.

'Yeah! Of course!'

The room erupts. Volcanic disgust. The answer they wanted. I'm lost.

'Wait, do you not?'

No, they say. Yuck, they say. Eurgh! Tastes nasty. No way. But girls put your dick in their mouth, right? Yeah, but that's different! That's normal. You're not supposed to eat pussy. Really? Seems fair. Seems enjoyable. In fact it was one of the first things I ever did sexually. I ate pussy before I penetrated. I really wanted to impress a girl and it worked. My god she loved it. Complete fluke. She thought I was a saint. Her name's Dolly.

Dolly ended up taking my virginity not that long ago.

White girl, curly hair, loves musicals. Has big boobs relatively and is up for it. A collectible at this age. Year above me. All the girls around here are white. You'll most likely find us with binoculars. A far cry from Neasden. I only started spending time with her because I got a part in the chorus of my school play. Which was a pisstake really. I was the only Black kid who auditioned and there was a main part written in patois. And I'm not shit. Teacher didn't like me. No word of a lie they cast a white kid called Tom in that part and didn't change the dialogue. Tom looks like he's straight out of a Beano comic. I hate him and I hate the school.

I got put on police suspension from school for two weeks, shortly after the play finished. There was an incident in PE. I said hi to a friend called Gem by nudging her on the shoulder. She said hi back but misplaced her footing. We were friends. That's why I said hi. The next day I was accused by her mother of slipping a disc in her back and ending Gem's tennis career. And the fact I'd said sorry when it was suggested I'd hurt her was seen as an admission of guilt. Before I was put on suspension, the deputy head teacher took me into his office and shouted at me. Said I was raised to beat women. Said I should write a letter of apology to Gem and her family. Stood there as I cried and tried to write it.

It became a police investigation. Which is ridiculous. But it did. And I was suspended. So that I didn't talk to witnesses. Gem and her mother would later face charges for wasting police time. During these two weeks I had a lot of time on my hands. I was happy I wasn't in school. Peak social years though. So I tried making plans. Boy meets girl makes more sense to me. I started texting Dolly. And we'd meet in the local park after she'd finished school. Sitting next to her was electric. Lip gloss and loose buttons. Dangerous combination. Flamenco dancer skirts. Tights. I don't know why I find this shit such a turn on. It's fucked up. Magnetic arousal. Living for the little moments. Lent back on one elbow. Eye contact. Thick mascara, curiosity and desire. She wasn't giving anything away either. Every time we met in the park, we spoke and then departed.

Got a text one night inviting me over to hers. Parents out. Best news. Alcohol. She had another friend over too. A buffer. Seemed like her family had money. Homely vibes. House a lot bigger than mine. Her room was fucking huge. Pictures everywhere. En suite bathroom. She was telling me that her ex was down to the last three to play Harry Potter. Apparently it was over as soon as Daniel Radcliffe walked in. The rest was just for show. We all got a bit tipsy. Then there was a moment when her friend seemed to wander off and her energy engulfed me. Her curls got extra curly. Her bed felt extra soft.

We kissed and touched. Rubbed each other. I was over the moon. What a body. Undressed each other a bit. And I just thought I'd go for it. Something in me thought I should go down on her. Slip down and lick for my life. Can't be that tough. I'm sure I'd seen enough from the thirty second porn previews you can sometimes get on the internet. I just went for it. Followed her reactions. Focussed on the bits she reacted to. A few minutes later she seemed incredibly happy. Still wasn't sure where her friend went. Her eyelids were a little low when she looked at me afterwards. Nodded. Like I'd got into a club. I suppose I had. A few weeks later, she took my virginity.

I enjoyed providing pleasure. Doing a good job. It felt powerful. Giving. Genuinely. It was never a question for me. And yet Big Hen and the boys are dismissing it. Ridiculing it. Unwilling. And they talk about receiving head as if that's the power position. Don't get it twisted. I was more excited about a blowjob than losing my virginity. To just lay back and be satisfied. What a luxury. But the girls have our penises in their mouths. Our sensitive sense of selves. I wonder if it's naive to believe we're in control at that point. Unless it's because it's pointed. That we think of our dicks as weapons. We have, after all, created guns in the image of our genitalia. Perpetuated a phallic fantasy. War. Carnage. And we back it with colloquialisms. It's an attack. We're the ones who shoot. We're the ones who fuck.

Still, the disgust breeds enquiry. Such a visceral reaction. As if it's a loss, to provide. The ridicule of submission.

Perhaps when you're more conditioned to value outcomes, you're less inclined to maximise the journey. Boys are always shouting 'suck my dick' at one another. Power play. Like that's the weaker position. Ingrained misogyny. Maybe it's what we want from other men and we're just angry about it. Doesn't even have to be sexual. Just intimacy. But it's intimidating. Intimate dating. A fear of rejection. People don't like things they don't understand. Would rather demonise each other than end up on the firing line. There is a lot of pressure to perform, as a boy. And providing pleasure involves sensuality. It involves communication and patience. But nah, we'll just call it 'nasty'. Maintain control. Mask the fear.

'So you just expect them to give it and you not give it back?' I say.

Shrugs. Yeah. Nods. As if it's the natural order, to simply take. I wonder if this exchange will make an impression on me. It's these moments that shape us in our teens. Good thing I hate order. Good thing I don't like being told what to do. Looks like I'll get one up on this lot. If I continue to keep pleasing. Don't have much rep to lose anyway.

And honestly I'm not convinced. None of these boys are convincing. 'Cause we're all posturing. Comparing. Competing. Sizing each other up. I hear boys at this age say some wild shit. In a bid to be alpha. Top of the food chain. And we're surprised why it takes us so long to figure things out. Sex and intimacy makes us all vulnerable. Temporarily.

There's no avoiding it. And vulnerability breeds connection. I bet even the most macho men have best friends who have seen them at their lowest. That's how brotherhood happens. You don't get it from two people fibbing out of fear.

Despite partially resisting. Not playing by the rules. Not buckling to pressure. I will go on to fall into many of the same traps, just from alternative angles. I will continue to go down on sexual partners. I will also use that, at times, to avoid cumming too quickly. I will hunt blowjobs like I'm shooting game. Ask for them. Angle for them. Get head in doorways. In parks. On roofs. Try and film it. Collect the experiences. Create currency. Estimate my own value in response. Have more sex. Hope I do a good job. Try and be respectful while not knowing what that means. Avoid relationships. Keep an ear out for promiscuity. Get drunk. Not remember things. Fumble. Misplace. Panic. Develop techniques. Deify. Gaze at pedestals. Of my own making. Experience what I think is love. Get high. Fall down. Enter hell. Avoid angels. Frown at the binary. Watch girls become women. Listen to them. Learn from them. Ask questions. Change tactics. Question myself. Claim allegiance. Remain avoidant. Say I'm this. Say I'm that. Stand out. Claim to be different. Say smart things. Not commit. Not grow up. Still go down. Still give head. Still brainwashed.

No, I don't become a lad banter lad culture take what I want then talk about it type. Yes, I continue to place an uncomfortable amount of my own self worth in sexual encounters. I struggle to say no to sex. In fact, I never do. I look for it. I convince myself it's all I need. Whenever a woman gets too close I ripple. Snake away. Disappear. I cannot be gathered. I dream of being a blur. A blur that gives then goes. I figure that's why I'm different. Because I'm not horrible before I vanish. I become a friendly ghost.

Yes I continue to eat pussy. But it'll be a while before I eat my words. Digest my shortcomings. Interrogate my fear. Stop running. Surrender. Know myself. Value my sexual energy. Value the time of others. Stop hiding behind wit. Know what I want. Instead of vibrating on beds. Next to lovers who want touch. Not untraceable edges. I will eat into my conditioning. I will tell myself that I'm worthy of love. I'm worthy of the word we would waste back then.

I will go on to lose contact with those boys. Consciously. Big Hen, Little Hen, Dylan. All of them. Our heads were in different places. I couldn't tell you when it hit them. The agonising evolution of maturity. Maybe it hasn't. A lot of man-boys knocking about. I've seen grown men still, un-ironically, use the term 'bowcat'. Big men with beards and kids. Still stuck in playground politics. Peacocking for the bullies. It's wild. One thing's for sure though. They eat pussy.

But it might take putting a gun to their heads to admit it.

# Eulogy

## Iggy London

**THERE WEREN'T A LOT OF BLACK FOLK THAT WORKED AT THE** law firm. And when I say there weren't a lot, I mean there were hardly any. A partner, a few legal assistants and an office manager who would waltz into my office unannounced and share weird jokes, usually at my expense. Occasionally she would try to get the latest tea that had pervaded the corridors the week prior.

The Water Cooler Chronicles, we would call it. Who was having sex with who, whose dad secured them a training contract, who got too drunk at the Christmas party and gave the Managing Director a lap dance. That sort of thing. Her visits to my office would always de-root me from the mundane world that I had somehow found myself in.

It was early 2017. Finally out of the comfort of law school, I was now working as a paralegal in a medium-sized firm. At first, I struggled. Whether it was the lack of daylight that came through the windows, the incessant loud noises from the coffee machine or the secretaries going toe to toe with the photocopier that always seemed to break down right before a court trial. I never quite found my place there.

Looking back on it now, the offices resembled the inside of an old casino, rather than a prestigious company that prided itself on its top tier legal services and fancy clients. Men in ill fitting suits. Misplaced wedding rings and manners, coupled with the stench of entitlement. This new life that I didn't understand in the beginning but slowly grew accustomed to by virtue of the fact that everyone else thought it was normal.

I had gone to law school, but in practice, I barely knew anything about law. Just thought it was better than being broke. I could only assume the partner who had offered me the job must've seen something in me that I didn't see in myself.

After some time at the law firm, I wrote a poem that would become one of the driving forces for this book. Around that time, I had bought into the dream. I believed with every fibre of my being that one day I would make it as a big shot solicitor and go on to be the next Louis Litt. I had dreams of marching into meetings and slamming settlement agreements onto tables. I'd be like Olivia Pope in *Scandal*— but with more sass!

But deep down, there was something that divided me from everyone else that worked there. A life experience that the people there had never seen or could ever recognise. An experience, which I had desperately tried to hide from them. Like many Black people working in corporate environments, I had to be careful to not show too much of my Blackness in the workspace. I had to be mindful of how I spoke, how I looked, what I said and everything in between.

My hopes of becoming a successful solicitor were spurred on by my desire for social mobility and the constant reminder that people like me didn't get first chances, let alone second ones. Admittedly, coming from a strong African family and having parents who 'in theory' wanted what was best for me, strengthened the need for this goal. There was an expectation. A standard—rarely said out loud but always implied—that I would reward my parents for their voyage across land and sea to give their offspring opportunities that they could only dream of.

I remember being 15, playing out with some friends at the local park and my mum calling me back home for dinner. She sat me down after handing me a large plate of jollof rice and began to spit bars to me that I remember to this day. Telling me that I had a shot in life, that I could be somebody. I would leave that dinner table completely confused as to what she meant.

As I grew older, I co-opted her words and created my own understanding of what they meant. To me, that 'shot' could only manifest itself in the form of a steady income, a job that I sort-of kind-of liked, a wife and kids. My parents wanted their son to be Uncle Phil from *The Fresh Prince of Bel Air*, not Chris Gardner from *The Pursuit of Happyness*.

So in 2018, when I made the decision to leave my profession and start my journey as a filmmaker, I naturally put a blip in that dream. Another fuck up, who couldn't keep a steady thing going for him. A disappointment that was in-between jobs rather than holding down one. My new career path meant sitting in Shoreditch coffee shops and sending random emails to commissioners with no replies. Going months on end without a film project and battling the rising cost of living.

I was left wondering whether this alternative dream of mine was ever going to become a reality. But like any obedient African son, I always dreamt of one day being able to pay my parents back. Every naira and pound spent on making me the person that I wanted to be.

After a solid year contemplating why the fuck I had left my comfortable job to become a permanent fixture in my mother's house, I stumbled on that poem I wrote whilst I was working at the law firm, conveniently titled 'We Built This Man'.

*We built this man*
*We built this man on white vest tops*
*We built this man in the image of Fela himself*

# Eulogy

*We built this man on spices and herbs firmly pressed by*
*mothers and fathers scattered on the poverty line.*
*We made this off parked cars and park benches*
*On hope, tightly squeezed between success and failure.*
*We built this man so far removed from the norm that*
*he is too close to freedom.*
*Built in the underbelly of the rhythm of the central line*
*Just so he could learn that freedom is wisdom in the*
*face of danger.*
*We built. We fought. We buried.*
*Built no man more deserving than the infant man.*
*Too broken to fix but too functional to be in pieces.*
*The infant man,*
*Born by unhappy trigger happy made men that left*
*suicide notes in form of love letters to the dead.*
*We built. We fought. We buried.*
*We built this man on those hands who still remain*
*accountable.*
*We built this man.*

This poem became the starting point for the conversations that preceded and inspired *MANDEM*. Reading the poem brought me back to a frustrating and melancholic time. On one hand, it had brought me back to the restrictive world of that office grind—half myself and half a figment of an imagined version of me that was palatable to the masses. But, on the other hand, there was another part of me that had remembered the painful events that had unfolded whilst I was there.

It made me relive it all over again. I reflected on one instance, in particular, when I was stuck in that office and received some devastating news. I desperately tried to keep my composure but I couldn't keep my work life and my personal life separate. As a young Black boy, there's a part of you that tends to block things out. But I couldn't contain this no matter how hard I tried.

It was a regular day. The same melancholic faces who seemed to hate their lives got on the train, staring into the distance or their mobile phones. I walked past the front desk, past the chatter at the water cooler and slid into my office. I opened up my web browser to *BBC News* as I always did. There, in bold print, I found out someone I knew had been stabbed and died. A man named Harry Uzoka.

I heard a knock on the door.

'When is the earliest you can get that contract reviewed for the client?'

The first person I ever lost to knife crime was a schoolmate called Ailton Campos De Oliveira. I was 17. Ailton was attacked in the early hours of July 4 2010 as he cycled home from a party on Tant Avenue in Canning Town, Newham.

Ailton, only 16 years old at the time, was attacked as a result of a postcode war—violence, often gang related, between those who live in different post codes. He died in hospital two days later following a knife wound to his right lung.

Ailton was one of the boldest, funniest people I have ever met. A joker at the best of times and a nuisance at the worst. Ailton's jokes would raise your spirits even if you were having a rubbish day, or if Mr Workmaster was getting on your nerves—yes, our maths teacher's surname was actually Workmaster. Ailton's ability to always see the brighter side of things baffled me. I know it is often the case to say this after someone's death, but trust me when I say, Ailton was special.

When Harry Uzoka, a 25 year old British model, died at the beginning of 2018, the band-aid of grief was ripped off and the sadness that I had felt when I was 17 resurfaced. Harry was a young man in the prime of his career, a role model within the community. Along with many others, I looked up to him as a source of inspiration and hoped that one day I could do monumental things with my talents, just like he did.

But this isn't just the case for me. For anyone who has lost a loved one, it takes a while to actually understand what is real. You receive messages from friends and family and you see images of them on social media but still, your mind and body cannot quite compute the reality of it. Eventually you see your friend's face all over the newspapers, social media, news bulletins, and you must finally face the truth.

2018 started the biggest rise in knife crime ever recorded in the country. The number of fatal stabbings in England and Wales in 2018 was the highest since 1946. According to the Office of National Statistics, one in four victims were men between the ages of 18-24. Twenty-five percent of victims were Black—the highest proportion since data was first collected in 1997. Although it is difficult to understand the exact cause of this rise, it doesn't take a genius to realise that cuts to children's and youth's services mean that communities like mine suffer the most.

The grief that is felt by those who have had to pick up the pieces following such a loss is unimaginable. The grandparents, mothers, fathers, brothers and sisters who have had to continue with this gaping hole is a true tragedy.

The tragic death of young Black men finds its way onto newspaper headlines often. The stories are usually the same, just wrapped up in a different piece of contextual ribbon. Time and time again we see these headlines and forget about the lives that pre-dated them. In the midst of this constant flow of propaganda, we forget about who these men wanted to be, who they were. We forget that they had families and friends—that they had a favourite show on Netflix or a favourite sport. We lose all of this when we whittle their lives down to statistics, political campaign strategies and tabloid chitter chatter.

There is a tendency for society to tarnish Black men with the same brush without understanding our true value and we in turn, at times, internalise these views. It is part of the reason why I wrote 'We Built This Man'—I wanted to stop feeling like I was to blame for the way Black men are portrayed in society. I realised that even if I became the best lawyer I could be, even if I was terrorising trainees like Louis Litt or slamming settlement agreements like Olivia Pope, it still wouldn't change how people saw me.

That's why this book was created. I wanted to be a part of something that would bring people together. Something I hope will change the way we think about the term 'mandem' and therefore how we think about Black men. What was once a term to describe a group of roadmen, is now used to represent a plethora of great artists, creatives and thinkers who have given their unique voices to this book.

As you have wandered through *MANDEM*'s pages, I hope you have laughed, smiled, widened your eyes in shock, perhaps cried, gasped and even screamed. I hope some of you were able to feel seen and heard. I pray that the vulnerability of the words in *MANDEM* give you solace and can provide you with strength. I wish that you are able to learn from *MANDEM*, and hopefully are able to see something in a way you had never considered. Importantly, for all who have made it this far—let's all do our bit to ensure the world can grow to be safer and freer for all mandem far and wide.

# Acknowledgments

It would be impossible for me to mention everyone who has been instrumental in making this book a reality, but it's only right that I try.

Firstly, thank you to all the contributors who have poured themselves into the pages of this book and offered their penmanship to tell such important and urgent stories. Thank you for the Zoom calls, voices notes and lengthy text messages. I rate you all. It's been years in the making and I'm grateful that you have all been part of the journey.

To Magdalene Abraha and Holly Faulks. Thank you for viewing me as a writer. For seeing the first draft of the book and believing in it. This belief carried me during the times when I thought I couldn't finish it.

To Newham for raising me. For being the only place that I would want to be from and represent for the rest of my life. Shout out to all the teachers and students that I met at Roman Road Primary School, St Bartholomew's School, and St. Bonaventure's Secondary School. No matter whatever I do and wherever I go, I'll never forget how you have shaped me.

But first and foremost, I would like to thank everyone

who has shared their story with me these past years. Thank you to anyone and everyone who has believed in me, the message behind this book and what it represents. Thank you to the Mandem.

# About the Authors

## ASHLEY HICKSON-LOVENCE

Ashley Hickson-Lovence is a novelist and Lecturer of Creative Writing. While working as an English teacher, he completed his MA in Creative Writing and Publishing from City, University of London and is currently finishing his PhD in Creative and Critical Writing at the University of East Anglia. His debut novel *The 392* was released in 2019 and his second novel *Your Show* was released in 2022. His third book is called *Wild East*.

## ATHIAN AKEC

Athian Akec is an upcoming historian, writer and speaker. His areas of focus are climate change, youth violence and racial inequality. He's written for the *Guardian*, *Independent* and other national newspapers. He's been profiled by *The Times* and was a cover star for *i-D* magazine's 40th Anniversary Up and Rising edition. Athian has spoken in the House of Commons as a member of the UK Youth Parliament.

## CHRISTIAN ADOFO

Christian Adofo is an established writer, cultural curator and author. His passion for writing looks at the intersection of heritage and identity in music and culture across the cultural landscape. His writing has been published in the *Guardian*, *Billboard*, *OkayAfrica* and more. His debut book is *A Quick Ting On: Afrobeats*, is a comprehensive book on the gripping journey of Afrobeats music.

## DIPO FALOYIN

Dipo Faloyin is the author of *Africa Is Not a Country* and a senior editor and writer at *VICE*. His writing has also appeared in the *Guardian*, *Esquire*, *Newsweek*, *Prospect*, *Dazed* and others.

## JORDAN STEPHENS

Jordan Stephens is a musician, writer and performer, perhaps best known as one half the chart-topping duo, Rizzle Kicks. Having been publicly open with his own struggles surrounding mental health, Jordan has been very active in creating awareness around the stigma. His mental health campaign #IAMWHOLE reached over 120 million people online and was mentioned in the Houses of Parliament. Most recently, Jordan hosted a groundbreaking conversation on mental health, music and systemic racism, as a collaboration between Channel 4 and IAMWHOLE to surround World Mental Health Day.

## JEFFREY BOAKYE

Jeffrey Boakye is an author, broadcaster and educator with a particular interest in issues surrounding race, masculinity, education and popular culture. Jeffrey, originally from Brixton in London, taught English to 11- to 18-year-olds for 15 years and now provides training for schools, universities and businesses on race, identity, masculinity and education. He began teaching in West London, before moving to East London where he established a successful English department at a pioneering free school, and then Yorkshire where he now lives with his wife and two sons. He is also Senior Teaching Fellow at the University of Manchester's Institute for Education.

## IGGY LONDON

Iggy London is an award-winning filmmaker, artist and writer whose work touches upon themes of identity, community, race and coming of age. Known for his distinctive style, his work crosses many mediums from film to poetry. His debut short film, *Black Boys Don't Cry*, which was adapted from a poem he wrote in university, investigates stereotypical notions of masculinity. He is committed to creating works that shift the boundaries of cinema, culture and beyond.

## OKECHUKWU NZELU

Okechukwu Nzelu's debut novel, *The Private Joys of Nnenna Maloney* (Dialogue Books), won a Betty Trask Award and was nominated for the Desmond Elliott Prize, among others. His second novel, *Here Again Now*, was published by Dialogue Books in 2022. He is a Lecturer in Creative Writing at Lancaster University.

## PHIL SAMBA

Phil Samba is a health promoter, researcher, social activist, and writer working in public health. His work primarily focuses on reducing health inequalities of people of colour, particularly improving the sexual and mental health of queer men of colour, and increasing visibility and representation for Black queer men. He's written for *Gay Times* and *Huck Magazine* and his expertise has been featured in the BBC, and the *Guardian*.

## SOPE SOETAN

Sope Soetan is a journalist, researcher, podcaster and music publicist. He has spearheaded award-winning PR campaigns for acts including Headie One, Ayra Starr and cktrl. He's published editorial work as a writer with *Complex UK*, *Mixmag*, *Okayplayer*, *CLASH* Magazine and many others. Interviewing esteemed artists like Patrice Rushen, Jazmine Sullivan, JoJo and serpentwithfeet. He is also a third of the music and pop-culture podcast *Don't Alert The Stans*, which has been endorsed by BeatsByDre and *BuzzFeed*.

## YOMI ṢODE

Yomi Ṣode is an award-winning Nigerian British writer. He is a recipient of the 2019 Jerwood Compton Poetry Fellowship and was shortlisted for The Brunel International African Poetry Prize 2021. His acclaimed one-man show *COAT* toured nationally to sold-out audiences. In 2020 his libretto *Remnants*, written in collaboration with award-winning composer James B. Wilson and performed with Chineke! Orchestra premiered on BBC Radio 3. In 2021, his play, and *breathe…* premiered at the Almeida Theatre to rave reviews. Yomi is a Complete Works alumnus and a member of Malika's Poetry Kitchen. He is the founder of BoxedIn, First Five, The Daddy Diaries, and mentorship programme, 12 in 12. Yomi is author of *Manorism*, his debut collection.